Truth Be Told

Truth Be Told

Tales from a Baggy Mouth

LINDA ROBSON

MICHAEL JOSEPH

MICHAEL JOSEPH

UK | USA | Canada | Ireland | Australia
India | New Zealand | South Africa

Michael Joseph is part of the Penguin Random House group of companies
whose addresses can be found at global.penguinrandomhouse.com.

First published 2024

002

Copyright © Linda Robson, 2024

The moral right of the author has been asserted

Set in 13.75/16.25pt Garamond MT Std
Typeset by Jouve (UK), Milton Keynes
Printed and bound in Great Britain by Clays Ltd, Elcograf S.p.A.

The authorized representative in the EEA is Penguin Random House Ireland,
Morrison Chambers, 32 Nassau Street, Dublin D02 YH68

A CIP catalogue record for this book is available from the British Library

ISBN: 978–0–241–62550–7

www.greenpenguin.co.uk

Introduction

When I've told people that I've been writing a book about my life, the most common reaction has been one of surprise.

Not surprise that I'm doing it — I've been around for quite a while now and have done my fair share of living.

People have been surprised that I've not done it before now! I'm known for my tendency to, shall we say, overshare . . . and so why have I waited until my mid-sixties and for more than half a century in showbiz to get it all down on paper?

What has taken me so long?

The truth is, I have been asked to write my life story before, many times, and I have thought long and hard about those offers. But when it came down to it, it never felt like the right moment.

This might sound funny given my *Loose Women* nickname of Baggy Mouth (thanks to my reputation for being unable to keep a secret and which became the subtitle of this book), but part of me wondered what on earth I had to say.

What would I fill a whole book with? And would anyone want to read something from a knock-kneed knackered old nosebag like me?

You see, I've never thought of myself as anything particularly special. Despite my job and being in the public eye, I'm not a 'celebrity' type; away from all the showbiz stuff, I have a very ordinary life where my family is my priority. They are at the heart of everything I do and I'd much rather spend time with them than hang out with famous faces at fancy red-carpet parties.

Being Mum and Nanny Linda to my kids and grandchildren is the most important role I've ever had.

I'm the same person I've always been – *Birds of a Feather* might have changed my life, but it didn't change me. I still live within a mile of the street I grew up on in Islington and I've never been tempted to move away. I can't imagine living anywhere else.

It's where my roots are. But more importantly, it's where my family are.

In short, I just didn't think I was interesting enough to justify writing any kind of memoir.

However, you might already be aware that the last few years have been incredibly tough for me and there were times when I wasn't sure I was going to be able to carry on.

A lot of people might see me on the telly and think that I must have a lovely life. They'll see how close I am to my family and that I've got a good job and a nice house.

All of that was – and is – true. And yet in the space of a year I went from being a happy, confident woman who had everything to live for, to a shell of a person on suicide watch in a rehab centre where my first thought each morning would be: *There's no way I'm going to make it through today.*

How did I end up there? I still can't quite get my head around it. But what I do know is that mental health issues can affect anyone at any time, and I'm living proof of that – I was sixty before any of my problems surfaced, although, looking back, they'd been bubbling away for a fair few years before that.

It doesn't matter who you are or what you have – everyone has the potential to get caught in the same downward spiral I found myself in, and I want to show that there should be no shame or embarrassment about it.

I'm talking about what happened to me, fully and frankly, because I'm a firm believer in speaking out and finding strength in numbers – by sharing our experiences we can all feel less alone, as well as help to break the stigma which still exists around mental health.

And now that I'm in recovery and feeling stronger and happier than I have done in years, I've reached a place where I'm ready to share exactly what I've been through.

I want people to know that there is hope.

So that was my starting point for wanting to write this book. But once I began delving back into my past, I realized that an awful lot has happened besides the challenges of the last few years.

Yes, I do have an ordinary life, but some extraordinary things have happened to me, and I've experienced the sort of success and riches I could only have dreamed of as a girl growing up in a north London council house.

There has been tragedy and heartbreak too. I've loved and I've lost and I've cried buckets. But I've also laughed a helluva lot and while writing about all of it, I've had the best time rooting through old photographs and diaries and having my memory jogged about things I'd long forgotten.

One memory tended to lead to another and then to

another and so there will be times when I veer off on a tangent! You have been warned.

Because of that, I suppose this isn't your usual celebrity autobiography. It's more a collection of stories – funny, sad and a little bit mad – about the experiences which have shaped me and the people who have made me who I am.

It's also a tribute to those people – some of them are no longer with us and I hope this book captures their spirit and how much they meant to me.

On top of this, it's given me the opportunity to set the record straight about a lot of things. Over the next few hundred pages or so, you are going to get the truth about my battle with alcohol, my breakdown, my marriage, my *Loose Women* colleagues and my lifelong friendship with Pauline Quirke.

But before we get down to business, I want to thank you from the bottom of my heart for picking up my book.

I've always had such a lovely relationship with the public and especially over the last few years when I've felt your love and support more than ever. You have helped carry me through the darkest days.

Some people say I've reached national treasure status . . . I think I probably have by now! All I know for sure is I've been a good person, I've got no harm in me and I've never said anything to be horrible to anyone. I'm honest and straight-talking and you'll get that from this book, I promise. But I've not got it in me to be nasty.

I just hope you enjoy reading about my life as much as I've enjoyed writing about it. It hasn't always been an easy process and it's involved revisiting some quite traumatic periods. But at the same time I've found it therapeutic to get all of it out there, and it's helped me come to terms with a lot of the trickier elements of my past.

More than anything else, I hope I give you a giggle or three at some of the amusing things that have happened to me, as well as the array of entertaining characters I've met along the way.

Looking back, I can't believe I've packed so much in!

Anyway, they do say that the best place to start is always at the beginning. So, with that in mind, shall we get going?

Childhood

In the beginning . . .

My mum always used to say that she had no idea where they got me from.

Right from the moment I managed to time my entrance into the world, just as the water pipes burst on the maternity ward at the German Hospital in Dalston on 13 March 1958, she knew I was going to be a handful. Perhaps being born on the thirteenth should have also been a bit of a clue about the chaos I was going to cause. But despite that supposedly jinxed birthdate, I feel I've been very lucky in life on the whole.

It's true that I was a bit of a wild child, though, and I've never done things by the book. I'm just not one for sticking to the rules, whereas my two younger sisters Tina and Debbie were always much quieter, primmer and 'properer' and never in any sort of trouble. And I've not changed really. I don't look much different either. In fact, I think I came out of the womb with this hairstyle.

My mum used to despair of the scruffy states I'd get myself into, especially since she was never anything less than immaculate. She was a fabulous-looking woman with the most beautiful skin, her dark hair held rigidly in place by a generous blast of Elnett hairspray, and with a slick of lipstick and her Max Factor face powder always expertly applied. She might have only been 5ft 3in, but my mum was a formidable force and she wouldn't leave the house unless she looked the part.

I, on the other hand, was forever scuffing shoes and ruining my best dresses.

Years later I'd take my own kids to school wearing a pair of slippers and with a big coat pulled over my pyjamas and Mum would be completely mortified. She'd say, 'Lin, I am so embarrassed! Whatever you do, don't get out of the car and let anyone see you like that.'

Sometimes I'd stop and pick up some bagels on the way home and she couldn't bear the thought that her friends might possibly have seen me. The young girls go out in their jarmies all the time these days, don't they? So I reckon I was actually ahead of the curve on that one.

I know I caused my poor mum all sorts of grief over the years. If she'd told me to be home by nine o'clock, you could guarantee I'd still be out at ten. She would jump in a cab to come out looking for me, scouring the streets of Islington until she found me, before dragging me into the taxi for an ear-bashing all the way home.

I was naughty at school too, always bunking off or getting into trouble for smoking. Once on a school trip me and my friends went into a photo booth at the station and missed the train back to London. When we eventually arrived back at Shelburne High School we got whacked across the legs with a ruler by Miss Butterworth.

And I remember Mr Lekala taking me into the toilets

once and washing my mouth out with a bar of soap, so I suppose I must have had a potty mouth all those years ago as well.

I told you I've never changed.

The Dardis family from Dublin

My mum, Rita Dardis – Reet Petite, they called her, after the Jackie Wilson song – was originally from Dublin and grew up in a tenement block on Pearse Street. She was one of thirteen kids – eight boys and five girls. There would have been fourteen but one died, something that was never really talked about.

There were only two bedrooms in their flat, so all the girls slept in one room and all the boys were in the other. My grandparents, Jack and Bridget, made do with a pull-down bed in the lounge.

I never knew my grandad Jack, but from what I was told he had some sort of engineering job and lost all his fingers in an accident at work. He got a big payout for that injury and bought a television with the money. This would have been around the late forties and it was a big deal to have a telly back in those days, so their flat would be packed out every evening with people from the rest of the block all huddled round watching whatever was on.

My nanny Bridget was known as Biddy and she was a big character, always looking out for other people, even though she had thirteen children of her own to tend to.

She wasn't a trained midwife, but she delivered every baby in that tenement block and she used to swear that you could tell the width of a woman's cervix by the size of her feet. Her theory went that if you had dainty little feet, then you'd be more likely to need a caesarean. The bigger the feet, the easier the birth, according to my nan. My *Loose Women* mate Janet Street-Porter has great size-nine plates of meat and I always tell her that if she'd had kids, those babies would have just fallen out of her.

She was very family-orientated my nanny Biddy. And she ran a tight ship; she'd make dinner and if you didn't eat it, then that was it, tough luck. Everyone knew fine well that they never got offered anything else, so it was a case of eat up or go hungry.

She was a fairly large woman, very strong and sturdy, and you wouldn't want to mess with her. You could say that she called a spade a spade and that meant she sometimes came across as a bit rude. I remember she used to give short shrift to taxi drivers if she thought they were taking the long way round. She'd go, 'JESUS! What are you going this way for?' while we stifled giggles and the driver winced. She didn't mince her words, put it that way.

Nanny Biddy's attention was always trained on her boys, who were treated like kings while the girls ran around after them and had to do all their brothers' ironing. I can just picture my own daughters' reactions if I'd tried to put similar rules in place when they were growing up. It wouldn't have been pretty.

Life wasn't easy for the Dardis family and it became even tougher in the early fifties when my mum's younger brother Noel developed polio as a teenager and became seriously ill. The sickness had come on all of a sudden and he was taken to a hospital just outside Dublin, while they burned all his bedding back at home, which was standard practice to stop the spread of the disease.

Polio was fairly common then – there was no vaccine until the sixties – but most people who got it did make a full recovery. However, my uncle Noel deteriorated and doctors told my nanny Biddy that he was unlikely to walk again and might not survive for much longer, which was news that shattered the whole family.

Noel was in hospital for about eighteen months and everyone would go and visit him, but he wasn't getting any better. Someone told my nan about this specialist treatment at St Bartholomew's Hospital in London which could help him and, desperate to give her son the best possible chance at life, she moved heaven and earth to come over to England. She packed their bags and left the Pearse Street tenement behind, arriving in London in 1955.

While Noel was getting treated at St Bart's, the wider family rented a place on Northchurch Road in Canonbury and would travel back and forth between Ireland and England whenever they could. They used to say that the house was haunted, and maybe it was, but they were all big drinkers and the booze might have had something to do with the ghosts they claimed to have seen.

It was during one of these trips across from Dublin to visit her brother that my mum met my dad and never went back.

I know they say opposites attract. Well, my mum and dad were like chalk and cheese and had nothing in common whatsoever.

Mum was nineteen when she met my dad and had been engaged to a bloke called Jimmy Sullivan back home. But she fell hard for Robert William Thomas Robson, known as Bobby, after they got chatting in the Jolly Farmers pub on Islington's Southgate Road, just opposite the house the Dardises were renting.

That was it, she was smitten, and poor old Jimmy Sullivan got given the elbow.

Dad was Islington born and bred and lived with his mum Eileen (my nanny Robbo) and his brother (my uncle Jimmy) at 17 Elmore Street, in a basement council flat which smelled permanently of paraffin thanks to the heater they used to keep warm.

Nanny Robbo had brought the two boys up on her own – they never knew their dad and he was never talked about. All we ever really knew about my grandad was that he was a chef and had a hunchback. Sometimes I wish I'd asked more questions about him because I do think it's important to understand where and who you've come from. Family history can help us make sense of a lot about the present, can't it? When your relatives die, they take all that unshared information with them and it's too late. But I never felt able to ask – it was like this unspoken rule never to go there and so we left it alone.

A few years ago I was asked to do the BBC show *Who*

Do You Think You Are? but turned it down because I was too scared about what I might discover. I'm not even sure what I thought I'd find, but I had a feeling it wouldn't be good. I'm kind of kicking myself now and I should have just gone for it. Maybe there's still time.

I know my dad's dad wasn't a nice man, though. Years later we'd find letters that he'd written to my dad and uncle Jimmy that Nanny Robbo had kept but never given them – one of them said he'd bought them a rabbit but it had died. What an evil thing to tell two little boys – it was like he was taunting them.

My nanny Robbo was a lovely woman, but she had a hard life and it showed. She always looked much older than she was with her tightly curled hair and National Health specs, rarely without a Woodbine cigarette burning between her fingers. She was also the first person in my life that I lost after she died of tuberculosis in 1965 when I was seven. I have a very vivid memory of seeing her coughing up blood into a hanky and she passed away not long after that, leaving a gaping hole in our family. I missed her so much and my dad was quite lost without her.

My mum and dad got married in 1957 at Our Lady and St Joseph's Church in Islington and moved into 23 Elmore Street, a council house just a couple of doors up from Nanny Robbo. These days the whole area has been gentrified and you can't buy a property like the one we lived in for less than £1.5 million, but I can assure you that back then it wasn't posh at all.

Plenty of my mum's siblings eventually settled over here too and Nanny Biddy never went back either, moving into a house on Culford Road, which was a ten-minute walk from my mum and dad. I think some of them who stayed behind in Dublin were upset that she never went back and I suppose that's understandable, but she was happy here.

When my grandad Jack died in 1958, she went back for his funeral, but it meant there was even less of a pull for her to return full-time. And in the end my uncle Noel lived until his sixties, so she had done the right thing by him considering the bleak prognosis he'd been given in Dublin. He was paralysed and so he never walked again but he was able to enjoy a really nice life. He learned to drive and had a little car to get about in and he also met and married my aunty Mary and they had four children together, so everything was clearly still working down there.

Noel turned out to be the brainy one in the family. He returned home to Dublin and became a jeweller specializing in those beautiful Claddagh rings. He was always making stuff for us and we thought the world of him.

My nan would go back across from time to time and she'd take us kids too. She was ever so crafty about it, getting the money from my mum for our tickets but secretly pocketing it for herself and instead making us hide under a blanket when the guards came around.

She never forgot her roots and when she died in 1983, she was buried in Dublin as was her wish. But London became her home and she made a life for herself here, especially when grandchildren started to come along. My uncle Sean and his wife moved in with her and she'd look after their kids while they went to work. At the final count she had over forty grandchildren in total.

It's impossible to keep track of a family that size. There are so many aunties, uncles and cousins on the Irish side, whenever we all get together, my kids spend most of the time whispering to me, 'Who's that?'

And I have to say, 'I haven't got a clue.'

The finest girl you ever want to meet

My mum had strong morals and a real kindness about her, but she could also be very vain and a bit of a snob. Even though she'd been one of thirteen, she'd been quite spoiled growing up and I think that gave her some snooty tendencies as an adult.

She would only eat ham from Marks & Spencer and she liked to take cabs everywhere because it made her feel quite grand. Sometimes she'd even take us to school in a taxi. And she sent us to Shelburne High School, not for its academic brilliance but because she thought the smart uniforms looked posh. They were navy blue with a pale blue stripe in the tie and they were really very nice, so I'll have to give her that.

Mum was small in height but sturdy in build. I remember once she was in the fish and chip shop round the corner from us and everyone started calling her Pat Butcher as a joke and she was so offended.

'Can you believe what they've been saying to me in there?' she said, all outraged. We, of course, found it hilarious.

She hated my Cockney accent so much that she sent me to elocution lessons to try and teach it out of me.

Given the way I talk today, you can probably tell that it didn't really work out. I tried it once under duress and then never went back.

My mum had some funny quirks which we never really understood, but she was unapologetically who she was, and she never changed. She didn't have a cup of tea her whole life, which was unheard of for an Irish woman. In fact, she only ever drank Diet Coke. I took her to Florida once and she could only get Pepsi and she was furious about that. She told me, deadly serious, that she'd never go back there again.

I don't think I ever saw her drink alcohol, even though she came from a family of big drinkers. I remember she was handed a Bacardi and Diet Coke one day and she spat it out in disgust.

I know it sounds awful to say, but she had no sense of humour. It's the same with my sisters; they don't really find anything funny either.

She definitely didn't like being the butt of the joke. She came to watch us filming *Birds of a Feather* all the time and the warm-up guy once spotted her in the audience. You couldn't really miss her – she used to backcomb her hair so much it was twice the size of her head.

'Good evening, madam,' he said, taking note of the bouffant. 'Did you motorbike here?'

Mum really got the hump about that. She didn't appreciate it one bit, but then she never saw the funny side of anything. Oh, and she hated Noel Edmonds. Couldn't stand him! No one ever knows why she took so much against him, but she'd say, 'Urgh, he drives me mad;

he's a terrible man!' Whenever he came on the telly she'd switch it straight off.

My mum always worked, sometimes in pubs, and she had a job in a cafe on Essex Road as well, but she was mainly a home help, going into elderly people's houses and doing their cleaning or a bit of shopping for them. She went above and beyond for everyone – sometimes they'd have a toilet accident while she was there and although she wasn't supposed to clean them up, she always would. She'd say, 'How could I leave them in their mess like that?'

She was massively superstitious, which was rooted in her Catholicism, and that's something she's passed down to me. If she saw a hearse, she would have to hold her collar until she saw a four-legged animal. Don't ask me why.

I remember I went to watch *True Grit* at the cinema on Holloway Road in 1969 and because I'd seen a hearse on the way there, I gripped the collar of my dress. So I was sitting in the pictures, still holding on to my collar, when a horse came on the screen. I thought, *Oh, that's a four-legged animal; it's not in real life, but it must still count*, and I allowed myself to let go. When I got home from the cinema, I found out that my cousin Lisa, who had spina bifida, had died and I blamed myself for letting go of my collar. I know it's stupid, but I carried a lot of guilt for a long time over that.

I still do it now. If I spot a hearse, even if I'm driving, I have to hold on to my collar until I see a dog or a cat or whatever because I'm convinced something bad is going to happen if I don't.

My mum never really had any friends, not close ones anyway. There was Beryl, Carol and Lily who she used to go to bingo with on Essex Road, and that was about it. But she wasn't interested in friendships because she loved her family so much. She loved us more than anything in the world – even more than the bingo.

And she absolutely adored my dad, although he was a dreadful husband. That might sound awful to say, but the way he treated her over the years, cheating with other women and staying out drinking until all hours, was shocking. He was never violent or anything like that; it was actually my mother who used to throw things. I remember her lobbing an egg at him once; he ducked and it smashed against the window.

Bobby Robson, my dad

My dad was a builder and a roofer, but he was a bit of a cowboy, truth be told. His favourite trick was to do someone's roof by taking and using tiles from the roof next door. Then he'd go and knock on the door of the house he'd nicked them from and say, 'Er, while I was up there doing your neighbour's roof I noticed you've got some tiles missing. Now, I can do you a good deal if you like . . .'

Honestly, he was such a scallywag.

My dad was a year younger than my mum and a right rascal. He was a good-looking man, not really handsome as such, but he had the gift of the gab, bucketloads of charisma and a great sense of humour, which I can see made him attractive to women. He knew it and, boy, did he make the most of it.

He was a real lad's lad and a heavy drinker, which was pretty normal in those days, especially round where we lived. The men would go out to work and then 'pop' to the pub on their way home where they'd stay for most of the rest of the night.

You look at what husbands and fathers do nowadays, going to every school play and attending all the sports days, and it was just never like that back then. My mum would always come and watch the shows I was performing in when I started getting into drama, but my dad? He was never there.

He'd be down the pub for most of the weekend as well. On a Sunday my mum would make a roast with all the trimmings, but he very rarely came home for it. He'd be out drinking with his mates, so she'd end up taking the dinner over to the pub and putting it on the bar for him. Sometimes he wasn't where he'd said he'd be, so she'd book a cab and drive around Islington looking for him, getting herself all upset because she knew deep down that he was carrying on and probably with someone he shouldn't have been.

Nanny Biddy had the measure of my dad; she knew exactly what he was like, and I think she worried about my mum and how his behaviour was affecting her. She'd question me, Debbie and Tina about what he'd been up to, probably because she knew my mum would try and cover for him.

'So, girls, has your father been out drinking every night this week?' she'd ask.

And we'd be caught in the awkward position of not wanting to lie to our nan but also wanting to protect our dad from her wrath.

Mum stayed with him because she loved him and the Irish Catholic in her desperately wanted – needed, in fact – the marriage to survive, despite all the times he let her down and cheated on her.

My dad loved his music, unlike my mum, and he'd play a lot of Engelbert Humperdinck, Frank Sinatra, Patsy Cline and Tom Jones, all that kind of stuff, around the house. He actually had a really good voice himself and if we ever had a party, he'd get up and do a turn, usually singing '(Up A) Lazy River', which was one of his favourites.

Because he worked on the roof, he always had a good healthy colour and he looked fit and strong. He loved having a suntan. He wore the same sort of clothes all the time – jeans and those polo shirts with the collar and three buttons. He liked to look smart and well turned out, and he managed to keep all his hair although it was quite fine. My sisters got my mum's thick, dark, Irish hair whereas I got my dad's.

He loved us to pieces, I know he did, and he was a good father in many ways, but he was never heavily involved with family life. We'd go to Clacton-on-Sea or Walton-on-the-Naze for our holidays and stay in a caravan and Dad would quite happily drive us down in the car, stop over for one night and then head back to London and leave us there. He'd come and pick us back up the following weekend. It seems strange thinking about it now, but we never batted an eyelid at the time. It was just the norm to us – the way things were.

I was always my dad's favourite. He used to take me to the Arsenal – I was there with him when they won the double in 1971 – and so we had a special bond. He'd quite often take me for breakfast before he headed home after dropping us off on our holidays, and I've found out since that my little sisters Tina and Debbie used to get the right hump that they weren't brought along too. This was long before I was on the telly so the favouritism was nothing to do with that. It was more because I was the first born, I think. Mind, when I did start to get a bit famous and the pubs around Islington put up photos of me as a local girl done good, my dad would go in and tell everyone, 'That's my daughter.'

My mum used to do that as well.

'You know, my daughter's Linda Robson,' she'd say to anyone who'd listen. Even my grandchildren have started bragging like that now, which is hilarious.

He always had my back, my dad. One night, when as usual I was sneaking back into the house through my bedroom window (having sneaked out a few hours before), my dad was sitting waiting for me in a chair, half asleep with a fag in his hand which had burned away to ash.

He woke up with a start. 'Where've you been?'

'I've been out with me mates,' I said. No point in trying to get out of this one.

'Well, don't let your mother know.'

Phew.

I was followed by Tina in 1960 and then Debbie in 1963. I think I was a bit spoiled, being the first born, and I probably got away with more than I should have because of that.

Debbie was the baby of the family and the most quiet and shy. Even now she can't for the life of her make a decision or do anything on her own. If it's going to a doctor's appointment, one of us has to go with her. She needs a lot of reassurance and has always struggled with her confidence.

Tina was Little Miss Perfect. Still is. If she said she'd be home at a certain time, she absolutely would be and probably five minutes early just to make sure. She's always been the sort of person who, like my mum, needs everything to be just so. Fussy.

I went on a cruise with her recently and I couldn't believe how long it took her to get ready every night. The amount of products she brought with her was unbelievable; her room was all set up like a poodle parlour.

Me? I'll just put a dress on and a bit of bronzer and I'm good to go. I have my eyelashes done professionally from time to time because I think that always looks nice, but other than that I can't be doing with the faff. I'm not interested in having Botox or fillers either. I was offered them for free once but said no thank you, mainly because if I start getting all that nonsense done then I don't have a leg to stand on when it comes to stopping my kids from doing it. As it stands, they know I'd kill them if they ever came home with those inflatable lips, the ones all the young girls have these days.

I'll just stick to my tried and tested method of getting rid of wrinkles: grow a fringe.

23 Elmore Street

Everyone used to pile round to our place because my mum had an open-door policy. She loved having a house full of people and if we brought friends over after school, there was always enough dinner for them as well, no matter what. It was a busy, noisy and mostly happy home.

My mum and dad slept at the top of the house and then one floor down from there was an open-plan kitchen and living room. The walls were all painted white and Dad had installed these black beams in the same fake-Tudor style of his favourite pub, the Oxford Arms at the top of our road.

The toilet was outside at the back in this little hut and we'd bathe once a week on a Sunday night in a metal tub by the fire in the lounge. In between Sundays we'd have quick flannel wash-downs of the three Fs – face, fingers and fanny – so we weren't totally filthy, but we can't have been very clean on just one bath a week, can we?

When Sunday came round, we'd all be fighting to get in the tub first because if you were unfortunate enough to be last, by that time the water would be unbearably cold. Even now it makes me shudder just thinking about it.

I distinctly remember the day my dad brought the bathroom into the house by converting the bedroom next to my parents' room. He put the bath in the middle, which was quite a trendy thing to do, I suppose, and there was a toilet and a sink. We felt like royalty having a proper bathroom, although it was still absolutely freezing because there was no central heating. We had this immersion heater which we used to put our towels on, so although they stank of burning fabric, at least they were warm.

That bathroom became like the heart of our home, especially as we got older. Me and my friends would spend hours getting ready for nights out in there, putting our make-up on in the mirror and chatting over a glass of wine. I think we spent more time in that bathroom than we ever did in the pubs.

On the ground floor we had two bedrooms knocked into one, which me, Debbie and Tina shared. I had my own little half and my sisters had bunk beds at the other side. It was at the front of the house, which made it easy to sneak out of the window, go and meet my mates (and probably a few boys) and come back drunk on Cinzano with my parents none the wiser.

There was also a basement flat, which my mum and dad used to sublet to people. A young couple lived there for a while before an old Jewish lady called Flo moved in, and if we were arriving home late at night, rather than wake my mum and dad up at the top of the house, we'd knock on poor Flo's door to let us in. She was lovely but, my goodness, we terrorized her.

Growing up, I knew money was tight, but we got by and I don't ever remember feeling like we were going without. There was always food on the table and my mum made sure we had nice clothes, not that I was ever thrilled about the way she dressed us. She'd put us in these frilly socks and horrible lace-up shoes which I absolutely hated. I used to hide a pair of plimsolls in my bag, get round the corner and change into them as soon as I was out of sight. On the way home I'd have to stop to put the horrible shoes back on again before Mum saw me, otherwise she'd have gone mad.

Puppy love

My crush on Donny Osmond knew no bounds. I was obsessed and the walls of my half of the bedroom were covered in posters of him. I had the purple hat, purple scarf, purple everything.

Whenever the Osmonds were in London, I'd wait for Donny to arrive at Heathrow Airport and then hang around for hours outside the Churchill Hotel on Portman Square, which is where they used to stay. One day, as he came out, he dropped a KitKat wrapper on the pavement (by accident, of course – Donny would never be a litterbug). I spotted it, grabbed it and it became my most treasured possession. I think I've probably still got it somewhere.

I truly thought we would eventually meet properly, he'd fall in love with me, I'd become a Mormon, we'd get married and live happily ever after. When I did finally meet him decades later, I told him all that. It was at *An Audience with Donny Osmond* in 2002, which was filmed at the ITV studios. The producers knew I was Donny mad, so they got me on stage and he sang 'Puppy Love' to me (and three other women too, but we'll not worry about them).

As he was singing, he was moving closer and closer to me and it was all I could do to stop myself from planting a smacker on his lovely lips. My husband and kids were in the audience and they honestly thought I was going to full on snog him.

I can't believe I'm even admitting to this, but afterwards I followed his wife Debbie into the toilets because I wanted to see what the competition was like close up! Not in a horrible way, I was just curious, and I can confirm that, as you can imagine, she was totally beautiful.

In 2021 I went to see Donny perform at the London Palladium and pulled a few strings to get backstage and into his dressing room, where I sat on his lap for a while. I asked him where he was staying and he told me it was the Ham Yard Hotel at Piccadilly, and I said, 'I might pop down there later . . .'

I think that's when his publicist started to usher me out!

They say you should never meet your heroes, but Donny Osmond is everything I hoped him to be and so much more. He's a gentleman and he's also aged really well. I don't think he's had any work on his face done either; I just think he's a prime example of what healthy living can do for you. He doesn't drink or smoke and I bet you he's never touched a drug in his life.

My sisters weren't that bothered about Donny, which was fine by me because it meant I had him all to myself.

When my dad went to prison

One of my most traumatic childhood memories is of my dad going to jail. The circumstances are a bit hazy to me and it's not something that was ever really discussed in depth as a family, but I know he bought a second-hand car from someone which turned out to be stolen and with fake number plates. The police arrested my dad and said that all he had to do was tell them who he'd got it from and they'd let him go. But where we're from, you don't grass, and so my dad refused to tell, the case went to court and he was put away for six months.

We were all distraught. My mum would go and visit him at Pentonville Prison, which was just round the corner from us, but she never took us girls. I don't think either of them wanted us to see him like that. But we missed him terribly and whenever we went to the All Saints youth club on Caledonian Road we would stand outside Pentonville and shout, 'Daddy, can you hear us?'

My mum, always wanting to save face, never liked to tell people where he was. Obviously everyone in the family and the people who lived around us all knew, but she didn't want anyone else finding out. I remember Debbie was quite ill while he was inside and she had to have her tonsils taken out. She told the nurse that her dad was in prison and my mum was horrified! She scolded Debbie, 'What did you tell her that for?!'

27

The day my mum walked out

For all my dad's drinking, womanizing and dodgy dealings, my mum stood by my dad and would defend him to the hilt. Apart from one time, that is. I don't know what prompted it – and we certainly never asked – but for whatever reason one day she decided she'd had enough and found something inside herself, some sort of strength or courage, to leave him.

I was about nine when she sat the three of us girls down and said, quite matter-of-factly, 'We're going to move to Lea Bridge Road for a little while because Mummy and Daddy haven't been getting on and we all need a little break.'

Well, I was devastated and started crying my eyes out. I didn't want to go and live away from my daddy; I wanted the family to stay together. But Mum wasn't having any of it and didn't entertain our protests.

That evening while my dad was out at work, we left the house, each of us carrying a hastily packed bag. Mum took the telly and all. She called us a cab and we put all our stuff in the boot and that was it. My dad would have come back later that night and found us all gone. I hated to think of that.

I'd left him a letter saying: *Daddy, please don't worry, we'll come back and see you.*

We went to stay with some friends of mum's over in the East End. They were good people but they lived in a two-up two-down, so there wasn't nearly enough room for the four of us to land on them and move in, but they welcomed us with open arms nonetheless. There was a pull-down bed in the living room and then two bedrooms upstairs. Me, Tina and Debbie shared a bed together, topping and tailing and never really getting a good night's sleep.

Mum got us into a school over there, while she found work as a cleaner and she tried to make it a happy time for us. But we missed our daddy desperately. I remember pretending to be ill so I could go and see him. I'd put a hot-water bottle on my forehead and then go, 'Mummy, look, I've got a temperature. I need to go and see Daddy.'

We did used to go back and see him on a Saturday, but it would only ever be sat outside a pub with a glass of Coke and a packet of crisps while he drank with his friends. Not exactly an emotional reunion or quality time together – there were never any trips to the zoo or the park. But all we cared about was that we were with our dad. It didn't matter to us where we were or what we were doing.

I don't really know what happened but, for whatever reason, our new life didn't work out. I think mum missed my dad too much. She certainly never stopped loving him. So, about six months after we'd left, she told us out of nowhere that we were moving back home. That was it. We packed everything up again, including the telly, and headed back to Elmore Street. And, very weirdly, this is where the whole course of my life turned on its head.

Because we'd left suddenly and without telling anyone, we couldn't get back into our old school, Rotherfield Primary, so we ended up at Ecclesbourne, which was just round the corner. At the same time as we started there, the art teacher called Anna Scher was setting up a drama club which ran at break times and after school, and me and my sisters decided to go along just for something to do. It was at Anna's that I would fall in love with performing and it's where my acting career began. So you could say that if my mum hadn't left my dad I would never have been an actress.

It's true, though. If our lives hadn't taken that brief diversion back in 1967, everything I've gone on to do since might never have happened at all. And a blossoming friendship may never have had the chance to fully bloom. Because joining me at Anna's was someone whose loyalty, love and enormous talent would change everything.

Hello, Pauline.

Drama Queen

A *Quirke* of fate

From the moment I met Pauline Quirke, we clicked. It was a firm two-peas-in-a-pod-type friendship right from the off, although we never realized just how intertwined our lives would become. And they remain so to this day, despite what the papers say.

Pauline lived on Ardleigh Road, which was the next one along from my nanny Biddy's. On a Sunday morning after we'd been to church all the kids would play out in the street, and me and her just hit it off. We both came from Irish backgrounds so there was an instant connection there (she always called me the Dublin Bitch and I called her the Tipperary Tart) and she had a great sense of fun with a decent amount of cheek thrown in for good measure. A girl after my own heart. Pauline was a happy kid and I just loved being around her. I think everyone did, because she was that kind of character.

There was only her mum Hetty looking after the three of them – as well as Pauline there was her brother Sean and sister Kitty – and they lived in this little block of flats with no hot water. We were poor but they were really poor. She never moaned about her lot, though. You couldn't ever just turn up at Pauline's house like you could at mine, though. Hetty wouldn't have that. I think because she liked to have a little nap in the afternoon and didn't want it to be disturbed. She worked in a pub and she was a lovely woman, but if you came round uninvited you'd be greeted with a sharp 'What are you doing here?' rather than a warm welcome.

So me and Pauline were already good mates but we became even closer when my mum moved us back to Islington and I started at Ecclesbourne, where she was in the year below me, and both of us joined up to Anna Scher's new drama club.

We did everything together and laughed all the time. We were never happier than when we were in each other's company. She was often labelled 'the chubby one' and I felt very protective over her for that because I knew her weight was something she was always conscious of.

I remember once sitting in a cafe in Chapel Market with her, having a nice chat over a cup of tea and lunch, when this woman who I'd never seen before in my life approached us out of nowhere, pointed to the chips on my plate and said to me, 'You don't want to eat that, you'll end up looking like her.' And she nodded towards Pauline.

That sort of thing used to happen quite a lot and I know it was really hurtful for Pauline. Obviously I told that woman to f*** right off.

Starting out at Anna Scher's

The idea of doing drama for fun, let alone as a job, had never entered my head. I wasn't what you'd describe as a performer and for all my mischief-making and confidence

32

I didn't ever crave being the centre of attention. And besides, kids like me didn't go into an industry like that, did we? Acting was for posh people who went to expensive schools and spoke nicely.

I started going along to Anna Scher's purely because it was something to do and it sounded like it could be a bit of a laugh. To me and my mates it was like having a local youth club to go to with the added bonus of some really good-looking boys being there too.

Martin and Gary Kemp joined up and they were always really handsome, Martin especially. All the girls loved him. My sister Tina went out with him for a while, the lucky so-and-so. She dated the former stunt performer Eddie Kidd as well when they were both youngsters, so she did all right for herself back in the day, didn't she?

There was definitely something about the Kemp brothers. They had genuine star quality and you could sense they were going to make it big. But they were always so charming and there was never even a hint of arrogance, and they've stayed exactly the same all these years later.

Martin came on as a guest when *Loose Women* celebrated my fiftieth year in showbiz in 2018, and he said that all the boys at Anna's used to fancy me. I wish I'd known that then! I had no idea, although I look back at pictures now and think I actually wasn't that bad. No one ever thinks that at the time, though, do they?

The Kemps aren't the only stars to have come through Anna's. Gillian Taylforth, Patsy Palmer, Kathy Burke, Phil Daniels, Natalie Cassidy and Jake Wood are just some of the others, which is an amazing track record and testament to Anna. It's all the more impressive when you consider she was an art teacher with no real acting experience. Funnily enough we saw her in a stage production once and she was the worst actress I've ever seen. But she was a completely brilliant teacher and all the kids loved her. She was only about twenty-three at the time, but when I was ten she seemed so grown-up. We were still in touch right up until she died in November 2023 and as the years went by that age gap between us didn't feel as big. I would bump into her down Chapel Market all the time and we'd go and have lunch in Ottolenghi on Upper Street.

The list of careers she launched is endless. The classes she ran only cost 10p but Anna would never chase people up for payment. She knew that a lot of families were on the breadline and she never did it for the money anyway. It was always just about us kids. And even the naughty ones totally respected her. When Anna said be quiet and listen, everyone stopped what they were doing and paid attention.

I was heartbroken when I heard the news of her death. I thought she'd be around forever. I owe that woman so much because I wouldn't be doing any of this without her. I wouldn't have had the opportunities to work, travel or even buy my own house had it not been for Anna.

She was a complete one-off. What a loss, but what a legacy.

Putting it into practice

Anna used to give us lots of improvisation work, which is what she became known for. I think she used it because a lot of the kids couldn't read very well and wouldn't have managed a script, so it was always at the core of her teaching. It put everyone on a sort of level playing field and, to my surprise, I found I was quite good at it.

What Anna would do was set the scene and tell a small group to imagine we were stuck at a bus stop, for example. And then she'd give you the first line, something really simple like: 'So . . . what are you doing here today?', which would set you on your way to creating a scene off the top of your head.

I loved all that. The off-the-cuff stuff is something I've done quite well throughout my career. If I'm ever on stage and fluff my lines, I never panic or get in a flap – that's the worst thing you can do because then the audience starts getting uncomfortable and it's hard to pull it back from there.

There was one time I was doing panto with Paul Nicholas and he appeared to completely dry up on stage. It was *Peter Pan* – I was playing Mrs Darling and he was Captain Hook – and he seemed to have a mind blank and couldn't remember his line.

So I made a joke of it and said, 'Are you going to say your next line, Mr Hook?'

'I'm thinking about it,' he replied. The audience cottoned on to what was happening and started to laugh.

'Have you got it yet?' I asked him, continuing the joke.

'It's coming . . .'

'Would you like me to say it for you, Mr Hook?'

By now the audience were loving it and that is always the best way to react to a situation like that during a live performance, especially in panto when none of it is really serious and you can get away with it.

Paul didn't see it like that, though. When we came off

stage he seemed cross with me and said something which is unprintable here.

I was a bit taken aback because I wasn't trying to make him look foolish. But I always had a good relationship with Paul and we did lots of pantos together over the years. When we were performing at Milton Keynes, he used to give me a lift back to Highgate where he lived and my husband would collect me from there. So that was very kind of him and showed he didn't bear grudges!

Child stars

When word started to get around about Anna's performing arts school, more kids joined up, so there were loads of us going along. What had started off with about sixty children had snowballed into a huge operation and after a couple of years she had to move it from the school art room over to premises in Bentham Court on Ecclesbourne Road. I think she had about one thousand kids on the books by that point and thousands more on a waiting list. Producers and casting directors had started to get wind of it as well, and someone from the BBC came down one day and ended up picking quite a few of us to be in a TV play.

I think us lot from Anna's were known as 'real' kids rather than the usual 'jazz hand' kids. We weren't thespians or theatrically trained to within an inch of our lives; we were just normal and natural, and so if there were ever dramas that needed young people who were a bit more rough around the edges, if you like, they came to us.

In 1970 when I was about twelve, me and Pauline and

a load of the other kids from Anna's were cast in a sci-fi type film called *Junket 89*, which was our first paid acting job. It was made by the Children's Film Foundation as a Saturday-morning pictures production where films were put on cheap for kids at the local cinema every weekend. I did a few of those over the years and they were always really good fun. In *Junket 89* I played a character called Daisy and Pauline played Molly, and we had such a laugh. We couldn't believe we were getting paid for it.

My mum and dad had never had a bank account themselves, but we needed to set one up for me to get my wages paid into. Back then you had to have someone introduce you to the bank manager as a surety, so to save my parents the hassle, Percy and Brida, a lovely Irish couple who ran the Prince Albert pub on Elmore Street where my mum had worked behind the bar, opened an account for me.

Me and Pauline ended up pulling pints at the Prince Albert a few years later when we were in between jobs. You had to be good at maths to work in a pub back then, adding everything up on your fingers, and the pair of us were pretty good barmaids although we preferred to be acting – that's where our passion was.

Another Saturday-morning-pictures film I did was *Anoop and the Elephant* in 1972, a comedy about a horrible circus owner. A thirteen-year-old Phil Daniels was in it with me and we filmed it up in County Durham. We told the other kids up there that Phil was Steve McQueen and I was Jane Fonda and they totally bought it. They all went home and told their parents, who must have been really impressed to hear that their children were working with the Hollywood A-list.

The following year me and Pauline got small parts in *Malachi's Cove*, which was a drama starring Donald Pleasence, Peter Vaughan and Veronica Quilligan. What a cast! We also did loads of extra work together on shows like *The Tomorrow People*, where we played schoolgirls who went to a pop show hosted by the DJ Ed Stewart. We just had to dance about in the background, but it was all paid work and I was getting a real taste for it.

I'd never really known what I wanted to do with my life and hadn't ever had a plan for a career, but now I had something I both enjoyed and was good at. And the pay wasn't too bad either so that was a win-win.

When I moved to Shelburne High School for Girls (the one with the smart uniforms my mum loved so much), I started doing plays in school time as well and Mr Hill, who was the drama teacher there, gave me the part of Philostrate in *A Midsummer Night's Dream*.

Mr Hill said I was performing it really well, but could I 'try not to do it in a Cockney accent'?

'Um, I can try, I suppose,' I replied.

I gave it my best shot, but I don't think I was very good at it. My accent range has never been much to write home about, but that hasn't been a problem to be honest because most of the parts I've had have been Londoners.

I can still remember every single one of my Philostrate lines more than fifty years on. My memory has always been good. I can remember lines from pantos I did decades ago and all sorts of long-forgotten TV shows. Sometimes I use them to check I've not got dementia. In fact, I've just tried it with my Philostrate lines now and could recite them in full, so I still seem to be in full working order.

How I matchmade for Tom Hardy (sort of)

Speaking of my Cockney accent, did you know it's partly responsible for Tom Hardy getting together with his wife Charlotte Riley?

Let me explain. I met Charlotte at the premiere of some film in the late noughties – beautiful girl, by the way, and a really lovely person. We were having a natter as I like to do with everyone at these things and she told me she was about to start filming *The Take* by Martina Cole for ITV and she needed a Cockney accent for the role.

I think she's originally from the north-east and she wasn't confident she could pull it off and sound authentic, so she asked if I would mind giving her some lessons and I said I'd be more than happy to help out.

We arranged to meet in Selfridges a couple of weeks later where we went through her script – I would say her line and she would record it and repeat back to me and she not only did a brilliant job on that series but she also ended up marrying Tom, who was her co-star.

They've got two children now and I like to think I played a small part in that. That's what I tell myself anyway.

A place for Linda

From the beginning and for a good few years after that Anna Scher was acting as my agent and fielding all the work offers that were coming in. And they were coming in thick and fast – I was never 'between jobs' for long. Most of the time I was going from one to the next, but I also worked in a fish and chip shop on Holloway Road and in a chemist and at a dry cleaner's down Hoxton Market on Saturdays.

I did *The Likely Lads* film in 1976 and a series called *Couples*, which is where I first worked with Maureen Lipman in person. A few years before that we'd been in a play together called *There's No Place* where she played my mum, but the audience only ever heard her voice. So we'd not actually shared the stage.

That play was my first taste of reviews, which I'd not really been aware of up until then. I was probably about fifteen and I played a runaway who was dossing down in this derelict building. One of the newspapers said, *There's no place? There is definitely a place for Linda!*, which I was so chuffed with, and I've never forgotten it.

That felt like a big deal and I suppose it was.

Teenage Kicks

School's out

I left school in 1974 with the worst O-level results known to man. I'd had a lot of time off for work and had fallen behind – we were all supposed to have chaperones making sure we kept up with schoolwork but it was never really enforced. I think it's a lot stricter with the child actors of today.

Mind you, I don't know if I'd have done much better anyway. The teachers used to say to me, 'Just because you're on the telly, Linda Robson, doesn't mean you can come to school whenever you feel like it!'

And I'd say, 'I used to come whenever I felt like it *before* I was on the telly!'

Me and Pauline were still as thick as thieves and some of my favourite memories are of the Friday nights we'd have down the pub with my dad and his mates. Pauline would come round to mine and we'd get ready in the bathroom, putting our make-up on and having a couple of drinks before meeting my dad in the Oxford Arms, where we wouldn't have to buy a drink all night. However, we were still young enough to feel the full force of my mother's fury and there was one night when Pauline was staying at my house and we came in late. I think we were supposed to be back at ten but it was gone eleven by the time we got in and as we opened the door, my mum walloped me.

Pauline started to laugh and so my mum walloped her and all.

Our big break

In the mid-seventies Pauline landed her own teenage magazine show – *Pauline's Quirkes* – and we couldn't believe our luck. It was hosted by the two of us and each week we'd do little comedy sketches and different interviews. And we'd always have a band on like the Bay City Rollers or Flintlock, an Essex boy band who were quite popular for a while back then.

I think we were the first people to do a chat show like that with a mix of light-hearted and more serious stuff. We did a feature on bone marrow donation where we interviewed Anthony Nolan's mum Shirley, who set up a trust in his name that is still going strong to this day. So we were covering important issues and the show did really well.

We were having the best time, although the entertainer Tommy Steele once rang up the studio to complain about our Cockney accents. Can you believe that? And coming from him, a Bermondsey boy who was born within earshot of the Bow Bells, I've never really got over the cheek of that.

Quite often the bands would invite us to go out with them afterwards and me and Pauline never needed asking twice. We always liked to party and have a drink – not that we ever got paralytic drunk, we just enjoyed socializing and making the most of this life that we'd kind of fallen into. By then we were old enough not to need a chaperone any more, which gave us a lot of freedom. Too much perhaps! We started getting invited to places, and one night we went to the Hippodrome on the corner of Charing Cross Road and got recognized by somebody who worked there. They gave us a VIP card which, to us, was like a golden ticket. We were like, 'Oh my God! This is amazing!'

It meant that whenever we went there, they'd get us a nice table and look after us all night. We both drank white-wine spritzers, which I thought were a bit more sophisticated than my usual Cinzano and lemonade that I'd ended up drinking by accident after going into a pub with my mates for the first time when I was sixteen. My friend had ordered a Cinzano and lemonade and I just said, 'I'll have the same as her,' because I didn't know what else to order.

There were never any drugs floating around. We honestly didn't see anything like that and I'm not sure why, because I'm not naive enough to think it wasn't going on. People sometimes ask me now if I've ever tried cocaine and I can say with my hand on my heart, I've never even been offered it. If me and Pauline had been back then, I think we'd have both freaked out and run away in the opposite direction.

If I was offered it now, I'd probably try it because the older I get, the more I want to give things a go before I die and miss the chance. God, my kids are going to kill me when they read this.

While things were starting to take off for me professionally, back at home it was a disaster zone.

My mum and dad's marriage troubles had always been there, despite the front they put on in public, and I don't think anyone could have described them as a gloriously happy couple. Maybe in the early days they were, before my dad started messing about, but once he started staying in the pub until all hours and spending time with other women, there was a lot of tension and it was always difficult between them.

And it all came crashing down one day around 1975 when a woman turned up at the house and delivered an absolute bombshell to my mum.

'Are you Rita?' she said.

'Yes,' she replied a little suspiciously.

'I just wanted to let you know that your husband has been living with me for the last two years.'

Talk about shock. As far as we had been aware, my dad had been working all day as a roofer, coming home, having a wash and then going out again to do a job as a night watchman. That's what he had told us, but the truth was, there had never been a night-watchman job and he'd actually been living this double life for years.

My mum was completely devastated. She'd turned a blind eye to his cheating in the past, but being confronted with it like this and finding out the extent of the betrayal was too much to bear.

The woman walked off, leaving my mum in a right

state. My dad didn't even try and deny it when he got back. I think he knew the game was up.

Mum chucked him out, and this time that really was the end of the marriage, although they never got divorced. There wasn't really any need to back then – it wasn't like they owned property or had any assets to divide up. And my mum would never have wanted to be known as a divorcee.

Part of me thinks she might have later regretted kicking him out because I don't believe she ever truly got over splitting up with my dad. To my mum it was as if she'd failed, and I think on some level she blamed herself, which is, of course, completely ridiculous. She was never to blame. My dad was the only one at fault, because he couldn't help himself.

But, like I said before, despite his many flaws, my mum adored him and maybe part of her expected him to come back to us.

He never did.

The woman who turned up at our house that day was the latest in a long line of flings and various bits on the side. One time we'd heard that he'd been having an affair with this woman Sue who worked in a chemist on Essex Road. Debbie, who as you know was the quietest of the lot of us, had been so upset that she found it in herself to confront this Sue woman. My meek, mild, wouldn't-say-boo-to-a-goose little sister, stormed into the chemist and shouted at Sue, 'You've taken our daddy away and we want him back!' So his behaviour did have a big impact on all of us and I could see he was making my mum sad, but we were distraught when we realized the marriage was over for good.

It didn't take long for my dad to move on. Knowing him, he probably had plenty of options. He moved up to Muswell Hill and in with a woman called Eve who he'd met while doing some work on her house. We didn't expect to like her but me, Tina and Debbie actually got on really well with Eve, although we could never let my mum know that we were having anything to do with her. She would have been really upset with us if she'd known and she never wanted to think of my dad with someone else.

In 1994 when Debbie got married in Cyprus, a destination we have always loved as a family, Dad brought his latest partner Jenny along as his guest and that was incredibly hard for my mum, seeing him with another woman like that, even all those years on from their split. She always carried a torch for him, but the last thing she'd have wanted was to have shown she was upset and so she put on a brave face for the whole day. We knew she was hurting, though.

Mum's new man

My mum moved on too in a way. She would never in a million years have called him her boyfriend, but there was a bloke called Johnny Bull who had been friends with my dad. I think he'd always loved my mum and when my parents split up Johnny sort of slipped in there.

We loved Johnny. We spent more time with him than we ever did with our dad, and I especially had a brilliant bond with him. He'd had a daughter called Lesley who was the same age as me but who had died of cystic fibrosis, and I think that made him feel very close to me.

He was the funniest man, a bit of an Arthur Daley type character, always on the make, buying things and selling them down Camden Passage. He'd had a tough life and had been put in Borstal for naughty boys when he was quite a young age just for smashing a window. He'd never really had a proper job.

As a family, we'd always known him, but after my dad was off the scene and living with Eve, he started coming around to see my mum more and more often and then eventually they just sort of stuck together. There was never any big announcement that they were a couple. They didn't ever make it official. It was a gradual thing over a number of years and they were good companions for each other, although, to be honest, none of us thought that my mum was ever really that bothered about Johnny. He was definitely far more interested in her than she was in him, but they would do lots of lovely things together like go away for weekends to Southend where they'd found a little hotel they both loved. That's the sort of thing my dad would never have done with her. I can't remember my dad ever taking my mum anywhere.

She did care for Johnny, though, and in later years she nursed him through his cancer before he died. He was in nappies towards the end, God love him, although that had the potential to send my mum's OCD through the roof. I remember one day we were cleaning him up – he was a big man was Johnny, so it was a two-person job, but my mum disappeared halfway through.

'Mum, can you come back and help me?' I shouted, my hands full of wet wipes.

But she was too busy running up the road with the bag containing the dirty nappy to chuck it in someone else's bin. There was no way she wanted it contaminating hers!

First love

A couple of years after I left school, I moved out of the family home on Elmore Street and into a flat with Tony Tyler, who was my first real boyfriend. Before him there had been a couple of boys I'd dated, but they weren't proper relationships.

Tony was the one I'd lost my virginity to. I'd gone to get the contraceptive pill from a clinic on Pine Street not far from where we lived, wearing a disguise in case anyone saw me and told my mum, who would have hit the roof.

I'd been sixteen when we got together (he was one month older than me) and I had fallen madly in love with him. We'd first met in a pub called the Agricultural on the corner of Chapel Market. It's still there, although it's the Islington Townhouse these days and a lot more classy than it was then.

He just came over to me and offered to buy me a drink (I probably asked for a Cinzano and lemonade), and we became quite friendly after that. I'd see him around and we'd always say hi, and I really fancied him.

There was a pub next to Anna's on Barnsbury Road called the King Edward where a lot of us from the drama group used to socialize and one night Tony was in there.

We spotted each other and he made a beeline for me. We started chatting and he asked me if he could walk me home and I said, 'Yeah, go on then.'

So he walked me home and then he kissed me. It was a nice kiss and I had all the butterflies in my belly for him.

He said, 'So . . . do you fancy going out again?'

And that was it.

He was really good-looking and a nice bloke as well. He was maybe too handsome for his own good because he had the choice of whichever girl he wanted, and that's what would be our downfall in the end as well as the cause of a lot of heartache. Mainly mine, as you'll soon find out.

Love and Heartache

Twice bitten

I've only been in love twice and haven't really had any relationships besides that. A couple of boys took me out a few times and I went to the pictures with the actor Jamie Foreman once when we were youngsters working together at Elstree. But I felt so uncomfortable about the thought of having to kiss him at the end of the night that I ran into the house and that was the end of that.

Tony Tyler was my first love and the love of my life.

After we'd been together a couple of years, we got a little one-bed housing association flat together on Barnsbury Street. Tony worked in a butcher's at Smithfield Market and so he used to come home every night absolutely stinking of meat. To this day I can't walk into a butcher's without feeling a bit ill. I can't bear the smell, I really can't.

We were happy together and I loved him so much, although he never really wanted me to go out with him and his mates, and on the odd occasion I did it felt like I was just tagging along. He was never horrible to me and we didn't have blazing rows about it, but he was a lad's lad and he liked his Fridays and Saturdays with the boys.

Remind you of anyone? Exactly. My mum used to say to me all the time, 'He's too much like your father, Lin.'

And he was like my dad in a lot of ways, not that I'd ever have wanted to admit that to anyone, least of all myself. Maybe it was part of the appeal, because I was always a daddy's girl.

I knew from early on in the relationship that Tony hadn't always been faithful because he'd admitted as much to me once. I had this friend – Jackie, her name was – who I knew from round Islington, although she was a couple of years younger than me. When me and Tony were on a night out, there were always girls going over to him and chatting, even right in front of me. Remember I said he was too good-looking to be trusted?

Jackie was one of those girls he would always flirt with and all this attention he would receive from other women used to really irritate me. It would drive me up the wall, to be honest.

There was one night me and him were having an argument about her and he revealed that something had happened between them. It came out in the heat of the moment, but he said it to deliberately hurt me and it cut deep. As soon as he'd put it out there, he tried to imply he had simply taken her lead. I wasn't having any of it. As if that made any difference. He could have said no!

That was the first red flag to me that this relationship wasn't what I'd thought or hoped it was. But I loved him and I wanted more than anything for it to work. So we patched things up and carried on and we were happy most of the time. And we were both ecstatic when I discovered I was expecting our baby.

A baby out of wedlock

To say that news of my pregnancy did not go down well with my mum would be the understatement of the century. She wasn't happy at all.

The thing is, me and Tony had been together for the best part of ten years, so he wasn't some flash in the pan. But we'd never married and that's what my mum focused on, because having babies out of wedlock was simply not 'the done thing' in an Irish Catholic family. Besides, she had only just about recovered from the horror of my little sister Tina falling pregnant at sixteen to her boyfriend Sergio a few years before, which had caused an awful lot of drama. And somehow I had found myself dragged into all that.

When Tina delivered her news, my mum had immediately turned to me and said, 'I'd have expected this from you! Not from her.'

Er, excuse me?! I hadn't even had sex when I turned sixteen, let alone got myself pregnant. I was so upset at that comment. I know I was naughty but I'd always behaved myself when it came to boys, so I thought that was really harsh.

Tina got grief as well, mind. I remember Nanny Biddy coming down really hard on her, and everyone told her it would never last with Sergio and she'd end up on her own. Well, she proved them all wrong and then some. Tina and Sergio stayed together and went on to have four children over the next ten years. They were always such a happy couple, completely in love and they built a lovely life for themselves. So it just goes to show that when the odds are stacked against you, if you love each other enough, sometimes these things do work out.

Even though I wasn't married, neither was I sixteen, and me and Tony had been 'living in sin' for several years, so should it really have been such a surprise that we were having a baby together? I'd been so worried about telling my mum and had been putting it off, knowing exactly how she would react. I think it was when we were all on holiday in Clacton and I was a couple of months into the pregnancy when she twigged that something was up.

I hadn't been feeling right and there had been a bit of sickness in the mornings, which, let's face it, is impossible to cover up when you're all under each other's feet in a cramped caravan together.

She said to me, 'Lin, if I didn't know you better, I'd say you were pregnant.'

I just went quiet and looked at the floor. Oh God.

'Linda,' she said, her voice hardening, 'are you pregnant?'

I couldn't deny it. I told her that, yes, I was, and she went into a mini-meltdown right in front of me.

'Oh my God! Oh Jesus! How am I going to tell the family that another one of mine's having a baby out of wedlock?'

I'd been prepared for her to be like that, but I was still a bit gutted that she clearly felt so embarrassed and ashamed of me.

My dad's response couldn't have been more different.

'Do you love him?' he asked.

'I do, Dad.'

'Do you want the baby?'

'Yes, so much.'

'Well, have the baby then.'

And that was it. Simple. That was my dad all over: straight to the point, no messing about. I told you earlier on that my parents were complete opposites, and the difference in how they reacted to the pregnancy was a perfect illustration of that.

Obviously my mum calmed down, and although she never approved of me and Tony not being married, she was a big support to me during the pregnancy and after I gave birth to our beautiful daughter Lauren Amy Tyler at University College Hospital in central London on 26 April 1983. And you couldn't have met a more devoted nanny to the ten grandchildren she eventually had between me, Tina and Debbie.

Trouble ahead

It was during the pregnancy that things between me and Tony really started to fall apart. We had moved out of Barnsbury Street by that time after organizing a property swap through the housing association. So we were living in a two-bedroom flat on Gissing Walk, just opposite where my sister Debbie lived on the neighbouring street. My friend Kiffy lived next door to Debbie – she's the mum of ex-*EastEnders'* star and king of the *I'm a Celebrity* jungle Joe Swash, and he grew up there, so we've known the family for decades.

Tony had started staying out drinking with his mates really late. Sometimes he wouldn't come home at all. It might sound weird, but it was actually the nights when he'd get back at 2 a.m. stone-cold sober which made me certain there was something funny going on. If he'd staggered in drunk, I'd have been hopping mad but would have accepted he'd been out drinking with his friends. Him coming home as sober as a judge was what set the alarm bells off that he was up to no good.

One night I decided to follow him. I didn't know what I was looking for or what I was going to find, but I couldn't live with the uncertainty any longer. I knew he used to go to a club called Riley's and another one by the Angel called Ra Ra's, which were the places you used to go to after the pubs had shut.

My dad's girlfriend Eve, who I'd grown really close to and who'd often given me a shoulder to cry on when I was upset about Tony, offered to come with me. So me, heavily pregnant with Lauren, and Eve had driven down to Riley's and waited in the car outside, just out of view as he emerged with a load of mates. We started following him, making sure we kept a good distance behind so he wouldn't spot us. After a few minutes we realized that for once he was heading straight back home. What an anticlimax!

He ended up getting in before me. When I came in a few minutes later he was ever so confused and said, 'Where have you been?'

I just made up some excuse about Eve needing to speak to me about something and that I'd popped out to see her.

He'd managed to dodge the bullet – must have been his lucky night – but I knew there was something going on.

The next week, me and Eve followed him again. This time he came out of Riley's with Tommy, who was going out with my sister Debbie (she would later end up marrying him), and neither of them were heading straight home like they had the previous week.

We tracked them both around to Lofting Road, where they went into this house. Me and Eve hid outside until we saw him at the window with a girl we vaguely knew.

That was all the evidence I needed. What the hell was he playing at with another woman when I was (supposedly) at home, pregnant with his child?

Suddenly overcome with fury, I went up and knocked on the door. I say knocked, but it was more like practically hammered it off the hinges.

Tony peered out the window, saw me and his face dropped.

'Open this f***ing door NOW!' I screamed.

At that moment I didn't care about the fact I was probably waking up the whole street. All I was concerned about was the fact that the man whose child I was carrying was sneaking about with another woman.

He wouldn't come down. I think he was frozen with fear, and he blimmin' well should've been and all. He called out through the window, 'It's nothing, honestly! I've just come to drop some football kit off.'

Football kit? At two in the morning?

I couldn't bear to look at him. I turned away and Eve drove me home, calling in at the kebab shop where

Debbie was getting some food at the end of a night out with her mates to tell her what had happened, and that Tommy was in on it too.

Tony came back a bit later full of excuses. It wasn't what I thought; he knew it looked bad but there was nothing going on. I told him I didn't want to be with him any more. I couldn't live like this. Most of all, I didn't want to end up like my mum and dad.

He was very upset and kept telling me he loved me, and over the next couple of days I suppose he just wore me down. I followed my heart rather than my head and agreed to give it another go because I loved him. I'd never been with anyone else; it had only ever been Tony.

So we muddled through and tried to put the relationship back together, and, to be fair, he did stop going out as much for a while. I was also really conscious of the baby in my tummy and wanting to provide it with a stable family unit. I wanted to believe that we would be OK. And I was scared about being left on my own.

The final straw

When Lauren came along in 1983, Tony was overjoyed to be a dad and he was brilliant with her. No matter what went on between me and Tony, he was never anything other than a great father to Lauren and they always had a fantastic relationship. But in the end that wasn't enough for us to survive as a couple, and while we did make a go of it for a couple of years after Lauren was born, I think deep down I knew it was only ever going to be a matter of time before he was up to his old tricks and it all blew up again.

Sure enough, one weekend in 1985, I came home from filming the fourth series of *Shine on Harvey Moon* up in Nottingham and found lipstick-stained tissues under the pillow.

I inspected it a bit more closely and there were strands of hair on the pillowcase that were not mine.

The rage boiled up inside of me. 'What the hell is this, Tony?'

Immediately the excuses and the lies came tumbling out of him. It must have been from a mate's girlfriend who'd stayed over, he'd never cheat on me, I had to believe him, blah blah blah. Same old, same old.

But that time I'd had enough. Maybe that's how my mum had felt all those years ago when she was confronted with the truth about my dad's double life and couldn't turn a blind eye to his cheating for a moment longer. From that point everything Tony had been up to behind my back all came out at once. I didn't know it at the time but his best friend Robert Warren (the brother of the boxing promoter Frank Warren, as it happens) had given Tony an ultimatum. Basically he had a week to tell me that he'd been seeing this other girl and if Tony didn't tell me then Robert would. Even though Robert was Tony's mate, he also felt a great deal of loyalty to me. He and his wife Linda had their son Bobby at the same time as I'd had Lauren and our two families did everything together. Lauren and Bobby had joint birthday parties until they were about eight and we were all really close.

Anyway, Tony refused to confess and so Robert told

me about this girl, which I appreciated him doing but it devastated me to learn that just about everyone in Islington had known apart from me. It was like the stuffing had been knocked out of me. I told Tony it was over. He had to leave. I didn't want him there any more. And he was left in no doubt that this time I was serious.

At first he refused to go, so I went to get his sister Jean who lived opposite us. I said, 'Jeanie, can you come over and get him to leave? He's going out all night with some-one else and coming home and using this flat as a stopover and it's not fair. I can't take it any more.'

So she came and told him to get out and I think he knew then that we were finished. He packed a bag and moved in with Jean.

Tony and this girl carried on their relationship and I'd see them driving up the mews together looking all happy and carefree. I used to stare out the window, play sad music and cry my heart out. In a way I wanted to be angry because I thought that would be an easier emotion to deal with, but I just felt this constant sadness, like I was numb to everything. I was properly heart-broken. I absolutely loved him; he was the only person I'd ever slept with and there's always something special about your first boyfriend.

The new girl was quite a bit younger than him – Tony was twenty-seven and she was almost a decade his junior, still a teenager, which I thought was a ridiculous age gap. She was just a trophy girlfriend to him, all trendy clothes and lovely-looking with gorgeous glossy hair. She led a glamorous lifestyle and made me feel like I couldn't compete even if I'd wanted to. I'd often see her up Chapel

Market and it always felt like she was looking down on me, which I thought was really pathetic.

My mum, who knew how cut up I was over the split and wanted to have her say, saw her in a shop one day and marched right up to her. She looked her up and down and said, 'I just wanted to see the *piece* that broke up my daughter's relationship.' And then she walked straight back out again. Reet Petite in full feisty mode. She was a class act, my mum.

Moving on

Sometimes I'd catch Tony looking over at our flat in a kind of regretful way and I think he did still love me. I still loved him too, despite everything he'd put me through. But we could never have made it work and I knew we were better off apart, however much it hurt.

Unsurprisingly Tony and his latest girlfriend didn't last. They split up after a few months and he then went out for a long time with another girl, called Sue. He seemed to really love her but she finished with him, which I was happy about because I don't think she'd ever really been that interested in Lauren. He ended up getting together with Jackie. Yes, that Jackie from all those years ago.

Me and her had what I would call an arm's-length relationship. We didn't have very much to do with each other but we kept it civil when our paths did inevitably cross. She was there at Lauren's wedding to Steve in Cyprus in 2013 and I was polite to her. I was definitely never horrible, but that was as far as it went with us.

Tony and Jackie stayed together until he died in August 2021. He'd been diagnosed with bone cancer about fifteen years previously but, with treatment, had managed to live with it all that time. I suppose it was always going to get him in the end because that's what cancer does, and when we knew it was time I went to see him to say my goodbyes. I'd asked Lauren to check with Jackie if it was OK for me to go and see him before he passed and she said that was fine, which I thought was really good of her. She didn't have to agree to that and I was grateful to her.

I went in with Lauren and Tony was in the bed. Lauren said, 'Dad, Mummy's here.'

I'm so glad I got to have some time with him because he died not long after that and we were all devastated by it. His death came after all the Covid lockdowns, which had meant he'd been separated from Lauren and his grandkids for such a long time and that made it even sadder. Before Covid he'd gone to her house every Tuesday to have dinner with her and the kids and so she felt they'd been robbed of all that time and the memories they could have made together.

I feel quite sorry for Jackie now after losing Tony and going through quite a lot herself. She still has a relationship with Lauren and the girls and there are certainly no hard feelings. There never were really.

Falling for Mark

It always happens when you're not looking for it, doesn't it? You think you've got your head sorted and then something – or someone – comes along to mess it all up again.

I'd probably been on my own for about a year and was happy to stay on my own for the foreseeable when Mark Dunford came back into my life. I say 'came back' because in the seventies I'd been his babysitter and he was a proper pain in the arse.

His family lived on Cleveland Road, not far from us, and Mark's mum and dad, Mary and Terry, used to pay me a couple of quid to look after his little sister Sam. But I had to keep a firm eye on Mark and his brother Paul the whole time because they were really naughty, always making a mess and giving me lip. He's a bit younger than me so I would have been about sixteen and he was thirteen, and I remember he wore these big bifocal glasses and had masses of curly hair. He looked like a mad professor.

Anyway, it must have been around 1986 when I was in this park with Lauren on Morton Road and he drove past, spotted us and stopped to have a chat. It was nice to see him and catch up with everything. He seemed to be doing all right for himself and had bought his own place over in Chingford.

As we were getting ready to leave, Lauren said to him, 'Can you give us a lift home?'

He said of course he could and when he dropped us off at Gissing Walk, he asked me if I fancied going out to get something to eat one night.

Well, I didn't really, to be perfectly honest. But I didn't want to be rude so I said, 'Yeah, all right then.'

I wasn't interested in getting into another relationship

at that time, not since it had taken me so long to recover from the break-up with Tony. I had started to quite enjoy my single, independent and uncomplicated life. I certainly wasn't hankering after a relationship or suffering with loneliness, and I'd definitely never thought of Mark in that way anyway. I was also a bit confused about what he was after – did he mean as friends or was he hoping for something more? It sounded like he'd invited me on a date, but I didn't want to presume that, and while it was flattering to be asked, I didn't know what he was expecting to get out of it.

A few nights later we met at this Italian place called the Sienna at Highbury Corner and it turned out to be quite a nice evening in the end. We sat and chatted like old mates, although he was dressed a bit strangely and was wearing a pair of those jelly shoes that kids wear on the beach.

When we finished, he took me home, but he had bits of spinach in his teeth from the meal, which I didn't have the heart to tell him about. I didn't want to embarrass him because I could tell he'd been making such a big effort all night. But all I could think was, *I hope he doesn't try and kiss me with those spinach teeth!*

I invited him in for a cuppa and Lauren was still up with my sister Debbie who had been babysitting for me. He played really nicely with Lauren, which I found quite sweet, and that was maybe the point where I started to see him in a different light.

He told me he'd give me a call, which he did the next day to ask me if I'd like to go out to dinner again. And when I said yes, this time I meant it.

Mark was always the polar opposite of Tony. He's never been a blokey character, he doesn't go out with his mates drinking (he doesn't even drink) and he's a total homebody. My mum wasn't so keen on him, mind. You know I mentioned before that she had no sense of humour? Well, Mark can be a proper wind-up merchant and he used to play tricks on her, which obviously she never saw the funny side of.

We went to Spain one year while the Open was on. We were staying in the apartment my dad had out there and everyone on the complex was talking about who might have won the golf – this was before the days of Google or mobile phones. Mark used to get a UK newspaper every day and my mum told these people she'd been chatting to round the pool that she'd just go and check the result with her son-in-law who would have bought a copy of the *Mirror* that morning. So she ran over to him and asked him who'd won the Open. Mark spotted an opportunity to have a bit of fun and so told her it was Bruce Willis, knowing my mum wouldn't put two and two together.

She came running back, delighted to be able to tell her new mates the news that it was Bruce Willis who had won the Open. And everyone erupted – I had to get in the pool so I didn't have to look at her, I was laughing that much.

My mum didn't see the joke. She thought Mark had shown her up and she wasn't happy. She said, 'He wouldn't do that to his own mother, would he?'

'He would, Mum,' I replied, still chuckling. 'The difference is she would find it funny.'

They did have their moments, though, and she knew deep down he was good for me and Lauren.

The wedding that nearly wasn't

It wasn't the most romantic of proposals. Sometime in 1988 Mark muttered something along the lines of, 'I think it's about time we got married.'

And I said, 'Yeah, OK.'

I'd wanted to do it in a registry office but he was adamant that we had a proper church wedding, so we got it booked for 25 August 1989. But as that date drew closer, it started to feel like it was jinxed when a series of events threw everything off course.

I had taken my mum and all the family to Cyprus before the wedding so we could get a nice suntan for the big day and while we were there we went out on a boat trip. As we were climbing off the boat, I slipped and managed to cut a main artery on top of my leg, right by my crumpet. It didn't bleed heavily at first – I was more concerned about the fact I was wearing this little white skirt which now had blood on it and looked like my period had leaked.

When we got back to the apartment, we tried to stem the flow of blood, but it just wouldn't stop. We knew I had to get medical help and so we wrapped one of my baby nephew's nappies round the wound and went to the local hospital, which, honest to God, was just this doctor's front room.

So there's me lying down on this bloke's kitchen table

while his kids were playing in the same room. I was screaming and the doctor kept on sending Mark away, saying he wasn't allowed in, which was making me even more distressed.

Whatever he was doing to me, it felt like I was being butchered. But he stopped the bleeding and when I flew home two days later and went to hospital to get it checked, they said he'd actually done a really good job.

I was recovering from that when, five days before the wedding, my mum's brother Sean died. He was the oldest of the family and the first of the siblings to go, and it was a real blow to my mum. She was so upset and maybe that shock was partly the reason for what happened next.

Debbie was still in Cyprus and my mum had popped over to hers to do a bit of cleaning ready for when she got back. Our phone rang and Mark picked it up but all he could hear was someone heavy breathing down the line.

'I think someone's giving us a dirty call,' he said.

I grabbed the phone from him. 'Hello?' I said. 'Hello? Who's this?'

Straight away I knew it wasn't a prank caller; it was my mum and she was struggling to speak. Mark ran straight over to Debbie's where he found Mum slumped in a chair – luckily he knew to get her up and keep her walking so that she stayed conscious while the ambulance came.

That was the first heart attack and she had another one when she was in the ambulance. I watched the paramedics working on her and it was the weirdest feeling, as if I was watching her from above.

Thankfully she pulled through, but she was in

intensive care for a few days and of course we had to cancel the wedding, but I didn't care about that. I just wanted my mum better. She was only in her early fifties and was as strong as an ox. I'd never considered the possibility of her getting ill. Thank God she managed to pick up the phone and we got there in time.

She made an amazing recovery and looked a million dollars when me and Mark finally married a few weeks later on the rearranged date of 16 September. You'd never know this was a woman who had just suffered two heart attacks.

She was on heart medication for the rest of her life, of course, but it turned out she had decades left in her. You'll have gathered by now that she was made of tough stuff, my mum.

We used to joke that because she never really liked Mark, she'd done it on purpose to try and stop the wedding.

Opposites attract

He's a grafter, Mark. He's always worked, even when I was earning silly money during the nineties and there was no need for him to. He's turned his hand to many different jobs and has set up and run several businesses including a children's bookshop.

He was a window cleaner when we got together, which some people turned their noses up at. I remember meeting quite a well-known actress at some event or other, and I was chatting away to her like I do with everyone.

I introduced her to Mark, she asked what he did and when he said he was a window cleaner, she honestly didn't know what to do with herself. She just said, 'Oh . . . right.'

It was a conversation-stopper in those circles, which is why Mark has never liked mixing in them. I told him after that incident that from now on we were going to say he was a 'glazing hygienist'.

Mark's always been good at looking after people and especially his mum since his dad died during lockdown. What he's never had any interest in is being part of my showbiz life. I can probably count on one hand the number of red-carpet events he's attended with me and he doesn't enjoy the celebrity parties I get invited to, which is why I've tended to take one of the kids or a friend along as my plus one. He always felt that everyone ignored him and so he'd much rather be at home.

I'd be out every night of the week if I could and love nothing more than a night at the theatre or having dinner with friends. Opposites attract? Well, maybe.

For more than thirty years we made the relationship work in spite of our many differences. But recently, for a number of reasons, those differences have become more obvious and we've both felt them more intensely than ever before. It's prompted some difficult and heart-breaking conversations about our future together and I'll touch on the decisions we've made around that a bit later on in this book.

But in any relationship there are going to be ups and downs along the way and even before our recent problems there have been times over the years where our marriage has sailed very close to the wind. One of the issues in the past was that we were like passing ships a lot of the time – he would leave to start his window cleaning at 5 a.m. and then I'd be out filming until late at night. And then when we did see each other we'd argue about how I was always working.

Mark's always been a fantastic dad, very hands on and willing to muck in, but sometimes I'd be getting in quite late and find the kids might still be up watching telly when they had school in the morning. I found it exasperating and it would blow up into a huge row when I'd only just got through the door. Now, I'm not saying I was totally innocent in all this – I know I'm not always the easiest to live with and maybe I should have cut him a bit of slack instead of immediately jumping down his throat. Looking after three children on your own is no picnic, after all.

Neither of us wanted to split up but in the mid-nineties that was definitely the way it was headed because we were stuck in this permanent rut of having a go at each other. By then we'd had two children together, Louis and Bobbie Girl, so there was a big pull to stay together and out of desperation I suggested we went to see a marriage guidance counsellor.

As Bobbie Girl was still very little, she used to come along with us and play with toys while we talked things through. Counselling wasn't a quick fix and I don't think it's what ultimately kept us together. But there was something about being able to work our way through this bad patch and discuss why we weren't getting along in a calm way with someone who was completely neutral that helped. We would take it in turns to have our say and the therapist gave us the space to do that.

However, the weirdest thing then happened. I was filming *Birds of a Feather* one night at the studio when our script editor told me that he thought he had seen one of his friends in the audience. He was quite amused as he asked, 'Isn't she your marriage guidance counsellor?' as if this was a funny coincidence rather than a massive breach of confidence. To me that was crossing a boundary I was not comfortable with one bit.

It put me off, knowing she was sitting watching me; it felt like a real intrusion. She really shouldn't have been there – it was so unprofessional of her and I was conscious of her presence all night. I'd opened my heart to this woman and shared some deeply private, personal thoughts and feelings with her in our sessions and now there she was watching me at work. Perhaps I should have asked her to leave but I didn't have it in me. But we never went back to see her again after that.

I can't claim that things were all hearts and flowers with me and Mark once we'd come through that sticky patch, because that simply wasn't true. There have been lots of happy times but plenty of rocky spells too, and in some ways it's a wonder we stayed together at all because, as I said before, we don't really have anything in common! The thing that has always overridden everything else, though, is that we both love our kids more than anything in the world. We have that huge vested interest and the love for our family is what has seen us through some choppy waters.

I've only ever been with two men – Tony and Mark – and they've both been long relationships. I know that whatever happens, I will never be with anyone else and I'm proud that we didn't give up at the first sign of trouble.

Career Woman

Funny bones

I've never thought of myself as being funny. But then people do laugh at things I say and the stories I tell, so maybe I am! And by the late seventies I was getting a real affinity for comedy and it had started to feel like this was where my heart really lay. Work was getting increasingly busy and I was over the moon to get a role in the sitcom *A Sharp Intake of Breath*, which starred Richard Wilson, Alun Armstrong and David Jason, who was fast becoming a household name having already done a series of *Open All Hours*.

David kept to himself; he wasn't larger than life or showy-offy like you might expect given the roles he's known for – he was much more reserved than that – but he was lovely and I liked him a lot.

In 1979 I got a small part in the sitcom *Agony* with Maureen Lipman again, who probably thought I was following her round by this point. She played an agony aunt with a radio phone-in show and it was the first time I'd done anything in front of a live studio audience. It's a different skill set to what I'd been used to because you have to wait for the laughter to finish before you deliver your next line and, not blowing my own trumpet or anything, it came to me quite easily.

The director said to me afterwards, 'Your comedy timing is brilliant, Linda', which was the first time anyone had remarked on that to me professionally. I was chuffed.

I did a series called *L for Lester* with Brian Murphy from *George and Mildred* and *Man About the House*. It never really took off, but it was all great experience for me when I was still only in my early twenties.

In 1981 I was cast in the Phil Redmond drama *Going Out*, which was a bit like an early version of *Skins*. Filmed in Southampton, it was about a group of school leavers who were headed for the dole, and it was a really good series. The director Colin Nutley went on to direct some of the biggest Swedish films of the nineties and obviously Phil is now one of the UK's most respected writers and producers with the likes of *Grange Hill*, *Brookside* and *Hollyoaks* under his belt. So I was well on my way to making a career out of this acting lark. My mum always used to say I didn't have a real job and I'd tell her it was real and I got paid real money to do it. Plus, learning lines wasn't always easy.

She'd harrumph and say, 'You're not down the mines, though, are you?'

Comedy queen

I found myself gravitating towards comedy again in the summer of 1983. I started filming a new sitcom for ITV called *Up the Elephant and Round the Castle* alongside Jim Davidson, John Bardon and Anita Dobson. Although it felt very early to be back at work after having Lauren, it worked out well for me because we shot it between

Elstree and Elephant and Castle, just south of the river, so it was easy enough to get to and from every day.

Jim Davidson played a lovable rogue called Jim London who'd inherited this house and got into all sorts of silly scrapes with the neighbours. I took the role of Cheryl who was marrying Jim's friend Arnold, played by Christopher Ellison, who became best known for his role as DCI Frank Burnside in *The Bill*.

What can I tell you about Jim Davidson? Well, Jim Davidson is Jim Davidson, isn't he? I think that's as much as I can say, to be quite honest. He had a real thing for Anita Dobson and he was quite flirty with her. He never came near me in that way. I was probably still carrying too much baby fat for his liking – not that I was complaining!

He wasn't a horrible man, but he was old-fashioned and sexist as you can probably imagine. Anita, God love her, could more than hold her own and didn't stand for any of his nonsense. She's a brilliant woman and a great actress and I still see her from time to time.

And I absolutely loved John Bardon, who was Jim's dad in the show and went on to play Jim Branning so fantastically in *EastEnders*. We stayed friends until he died in 2014. The last time I saw him was down at the *EastEnders* set; he was in a wheelchair and couldn't speak and he got really emotional. It broke my heart to see him like that.

Shooting with the stars

When you're starting out as an actress, landing a part – however small – alongside a genuine A-lister is a real thrill.

In the late seventies I found myself playing a dinner lady on the set of the movie *Absolution* starring the late, great Richard Burton and Billy Connolly, who wasn't as famous then as he is now.

Richard's scenes were done with a stand-in until it was time to shoot and he would appear from nowhere, do his thing and disappear again. When you get to that level, you don't do the donkey work. My scenes were with an actress called Hilda Fenemore who played the cook and we were picked up from the hotel together each morning and brought to the set where we shared a Winnebago.

We had cups of tea with Billy in between scenes and he was the nicest bloke – funny and generous and full of stories, just as you'd expect. One day, when it was time to head back to the hotel, me and Hilda went and sat in the back of a waiting car, assuming it was our lift. A panicked member of production came running over. 'This is Mr Burton's car!' he said. 'Can you please get out?!' Me and Hilda looked at each other and clapped our hands over our mouths. Flushed with embarrassment, we clambered back out of the car again, trying not to wet ourselves laughing. The shame!

Snooty behaviour

I was always confident as a young woman, but there were times I was a bit overawed by certain people. I look back now and wish I'd stood up for myself in certain situations. I did Agatha Christie's *The Case of the Middle-Aged Wife* as part of a TV mini-series and the cast was full of Shakespearean actors so I already felt a bit of a fish out of water. Gwen Watford and Peter Jones were in it and they were proper famous in those days and well established.

In the programme, their characters had a restaurant and I was one of the kitchen workers, but even when the cameras stopped rolling they treated me and the other younger cast members as if we were actually there to wait on them. So at lunchtime they'd send us off to run along and fetch their sandwiches from Marks & Spencer and I used to do it even though it really, really annoyed me.

Peter Jones would even speak to me with a Cockney accent – a really bad one, as it happens – to mock me and I had to pretend to laugh it off, but I was seething inside. So rude! Just because they were posher than the rest of us, they thought that was OK. They were upstairs and we were downstairs, and we went along with it because we thought we had to.

I wouldn't put up with that rubbish now and if I ever see anyone behaving like that wherever I am and whoever they are, I'll step in and call it out. I can't stand that sort of thing. And if I could go back in time I'd say to Gwen and Peter: 'Go and get your own f***ing sandwich!'

Finding my voice

There was an incident around the same time where I very much did find my voice when I needed it. It was 1982 and I was playing Theresa McCorrigan in a gritty mini-series about the IRA called *Harry's Game*, which was the first time

I'd done anything with a different accent. Mr Hill at Shelburne High would have been pleased. Tommy Steele too.

I was really nervous about getting it right, but my mum's friend Beryl from the bingo was from Northern Ireland and she helped me out with it. She told me it sounded good so that reassured me.

My character Theresa was a bit of an IRA groupie and there was a scene where I had to get into bed with the actor Derek Thompson, who you'll know because he went on to be a *Casualty* legend as Charlie Fairhead. I was already a bit traumatized at the thought of doing a bedroom scene – I don't know anyone in the business who looks forward to them – when I was asked in front of the whole studio with all the production staff, wardrobe, hair and make-up watching on if I could take off my nightdress.

No quiet word in my ear, no sensitive discussion about what I'd be comfortable with. Just me being put on the spot about doing a naked scene with everyone standing there gawping.

I felt disgusted and said, 'F*** off!' And all the crew started clapping because they knew it was bang out of order.

The absolute cheek! The script had never suggested anything of the sort. If I had been asked in private how I felt about it, I'd have still said no, but it wouldn't have been so humiliating. After that I got quite good at standing up for myself, but I can see how other actresses who aren't as gobby as me would have easily ended up railroaded into situations they weren't comfortable with.

That was the only time I had anything like that happen

and I'm relieved that I never experienced any of the casting-couch behaviour we now know was rife at the time and for years to come.

However, there was once a producer who I had known for a long time – I don't want to name anyone but I'd worked with him for a number of years and we had a really good relationship. I trusted him and we were close. We were all on a boat after filming one evening. We'd all been drinking wine and everyone was having a good time, until I found myself on my own with him in one of the rooms.

I felt the atmosphere turn a bit funny and he made a pass by sort of jumping up and lunging at me.

Despite the alcohol, I reacted quickly and pushed him off. 'What the f*** are you doing?' I asked him in complete shock.

I ran out of the room, very upset, because I'd never have thought in a million years that he'd do anything like that.

He apologized to me the next day, blaming it on having had too much to drink, and I told him to just forget about it, but I've never felt the same about him since. It was the only time in my career that a man had done anything like that, and what made it even worse was that I'd always thought he was such a nice person. Maybe it taught me that you can never really know anyone.

My time to 'shine'

All in all, work was busy in the early eighties and I was earning quite decent money, but it was *Shine on Harvey*

Moon which proved to be my biggest break to date. And for reasons which went way beyond the show itself.

If you're as old as me, you'll remember that the series was set in the East End of London shortly after the Second World War. And it was written by Laurence Marks and Maurice Gran, who would go on to write a certain sitcom a few years later about two sisters whose husbands were banged up for armed robbery . . .

I played Maggie Moon who was quite prudish but had a good heart. They filmed the first series in 1981 up at Elstree Studios in Hertfordshire, just north of London, which was perfect for me travelling in. They were fantastic days because I loved the show and the cast were so tight-knit with each other. Lee Whitlock played my little brother and he was great – we kept in touch for years after the show finished. I was also very close to Maggie Steed who played my mum Rita, and I still see Kenneth Cranham who played Harvey because he lives in Islington too and I always love catching up with him.

It went to air on ITV in January 1982 and a second series was commissioned before the first had even finished. We were absolutely delighted and filming started up again really quickly in order to get series two out that September.

They moved the third series from Elstree up to Nottingham, which meant staying up there from Monday to Friday during filming. I had Lauren by then and couldn't leave her behind in London while she was still a baby, so I had no choice but to take her with me.

My mum would get the train up to Nottingham with

us every Monday morning and look after her while I was at work. She'd stay in the hotel with us and spend the week taking Lauren out for walks in the pushchair, and just knowing my baby was in the safest of hands allowed me to concentrate on the job. We came back to London every weekend, but it was so good of my mum to do that for me because it was a big ask and there's no way I could have done that third series without her. *Shine on Harvey Moon* was a huge show which I loved doing. I was also at a key point in my career where I was getting quite established and so it could have been really damaging to my future if I'd been forced to walk away.

The writers Laurence and Maurice came up with the idea of getting Lauren into an episode, since she was there and available! I loved that because it would be something to keep for ever and show her on video when she was older. Anyway, Elizabeth Spriggs, who played my nan was lovely but she was this very Shakespearean actress and she could be quite loud and scary. She'd brought this big cuddly toy cat in for Lauren and just before we were due to start filming, she took it over to her in the pram and boomed, 'HELLOOOOO!' really loudly right in her face.

Lauren immediately burst out crying. She didn't like Elizabeth very much after that, which was unfortunate because all her scenes were with her and that meant she screamed the entire time. I'd seen babies bawling their eyes out on telly dramas before, and I'd always think what a terrible mum they must have, letting them scream like that. That'll teach me, won't it?

Three's a crowd

Lauren wasn't the only one who was hurriedly written into the scripts at the last minute. Pauline came up to visit me in Nottingham one night and ended up getting a part for the last few episodes of series three. She got kept on for the fourth series as well, so she must have done all right!

What happened was, we were all in the bar after work having a bit of a laugh and Laurence and Maurice came up with the idea of writing a part for her. Pauline was up for it and so the character Veronica was created, and she stayed on in Nottingham to film. This was before she had kids so she could be flexible with her time.

But you know the saying 'two's company, three's a crowd'? That's kind of what happened with me, Pauline and my friend Michele Winstanley who played Janice.

Michele had come from Anna Scher's too, so me and her went way back and were really good mates. We'd also done that Phil Redmond series *Going Out* together. But Pauline and Michele didn't really get on. Maybe it was a jealousy thing, I don't know, but they were quite different people and so it probably boiled down to a clash of personalities.

I remember Pauline had run herself a lovely bubble bath in the hotel at the end of a long day's filming and she was getting ready for a soak. Well, Michele breezes into the room, spots the freshly run bath, gets herself undressed and climbs into it without a care in the world. She didn't even ask.

Pauline's jaw dropped to the floor at the cheek of her. She looked at me in complete disbelief but I couldn't say anything because I was too busy laughing.

''Ere! Are you an only child?!' yelled Pauline in the direction of the bathroom.

But Michele was oblivious to what was going on and clearly thoroughly enjoying her nice hot bubble bath. It still makes me giggle thinking about it now and the look on Pauline's face. Michele was a lovely girl but she didn't half wind Pauline up.

In the end I was quite pleased when Michele finished her filming early and went back to London, because it was starting to get a bit tense between the two of them, and I was always the one stuck in the middle.

Celebrity mingling

The high-profile jobs also meant that me and Pauline continued to get nice perks here and there, which we were happy to take full advantage of, thank you very much! We especially loved going to Stringfellows in London's Covent Garden where Peter Stringfellow always looked after us really well. He'd make sure we got a good table and would send over bottles of wine. We were treated like royalty. We used to like watching all the celebs on their nights out. We once spotted George Michael and that was a real thrill, although we didn't dare go over and talk to him.

I did, however, touch him.

He was with Kathy Jeung, who was his girlfriend at the

time – this was long before he finally came out at gay in the late nineties – but I managed to sidle up to him and stroke his arm. A lovely arm it was too.

'You'll get us chucked out!' scolded Pauline through gritted teeth. She just about died of embarrassment.

We had such great times back then, just a couple of jobbing actresses from north London, making the most of whatever came our way. Neither of us had any clue that there was something just round the corner that was about to change our lives for ever.

Can you guess what that might have been?

Birds of a Feather

What'll I do?

If I was to write down all the things that *Birds of a Feather* has given me, I'd fill the rest of this book. I can't begin to tell you what that show has done for me in every aspect of my life. And people still love it, so it really has stood the test of time. Channel 5 did a documentary in 2023 called *Thirty Years of Laughs* with loads of old clips and it was quite emotional sitting watching that. Just happy memories of good times mucking about and, of course, getting into trouble.

The characters were so well written and viewers felt like they knew them. They don't seem to make comedies like that any more, perhaps because everything has to be politically correct these days. *Fawlty Towers* would probably be seen as too controversial to be made today.

At the time *Birds* came along work was very healthy for me. It was the late eighties and I'd just finished filming the *EastEnders* flashback spin-off *CivvyStreet*, which was set in the Second World War, when I got the call that would change everything.

Laurence Marks and Maurice Gran, who had written *Shine on Harvey Moon* as well as Rik Mayall's sitcom *The New Statesman* (a talented duo!), got in touch with me and Pauline and said they'd like to discuss a new show with us both. They'd been saying for a couple of years that they'd wanted to write something for the two of us after seeing us make all the crew laugh in between takes on *Harvey Moon* with these little improvised sketches. They said they liked the chemistry we had, but I don't think we ever expected anything to come of it. They'd once pitched some idea about a show set on a scrapyard which we'd quite liked but it never really went anywhere.

So this day we went to meet them for lunch in Islington and they said they'd come up with something they thought was a winner. It was a sitcom about two sisters whose husbands were in prison for armed robbery. They'd come up with the concept when they'd been staying in a hotel over Christmas and had overheard these two women talking about their husbands who were in prison and the idea had gone from there.

The more they told us about this series they were writing, the more I loved it. They said one of the sisters would live in a million-pound house in Chigwell while the other was in a high-rise block of flats in Edmonton and Pauline rolled her eyes and said jokingly, 'Well, I know which sister *I* am . . .'

Meeting Lesley

Laurence and Maurice mentioned a third main character who was larger than life and lived next door to the sister with the house in Chigwell. They already had Lesley Joseph in mind to play her, who they really wanted us to meet and so a table was booked for the Ritz – the Ritz! – the following week.

Me and Pauline turned up really inappropriately dressed considering we were lunching at one of the classiest and most upmarket places in London. She had a pair of old Reebok trainers on and I was in my sloppy casual gear. I haven't got a clue why we didn't make more of an effort but it wasn't in either of our natures to get dolled up.

As the waiter led us to the table, weaving our way through all the fine diners quaffing their champagne, we saw Lesley was already there looking completely glamorous with her big hair and brightly painted nails. What she must have thought of us two lolloping towards her I have no idea, but she didn't flinch.

We sat down and said our hellos as Laurence and Maurice did the introductions and the wine waiter came over with an expensive bottle of pink champagne. He poured it in our flutes and then me and Pauline, not knowing any better, immediately added sparkling water to it. The waiter was clearly horrified, although of course he never commented. We just liked our spritzers!

On paper the three of us should never have been friends, but there was something between me, Pauline and Lesley that just clicked. Laurence and Maurice had felt it would work before we'd even met and they were absolutely right. From that very first meeting we got on like a house on fire and you could say it was at the Ritz that Tracey Stubbs, Sharon Theodopolopodous and Dorien Green were born.

Things moved really quickly after that, and a few weeks later when we saw the finished *Birds of a Feather* scripts and how funny they were, we couldn't wait to get started.

Here we go.

And so it begins . . .

We might have been about to star in a BBC sitcom written especially for us, but if me and Pauline thought we were about to start living the high life we could think again. On the first day of filming, there wasn't a car sent to pick us up as you'd probably expect and we definitely weren't the hoity-toity sort to demand anything like that. Instead, we got the bus all the way across London from Islington to White City, s***ting ourselves for the whole journey worrying about whether we were going to be able to pull this off. I'd done plenty of comedies before this but only in a supporting role – this was the first time I was taking on the lead and I felt the weight of that pressure.

We had a week of rehearsals which went really well, and so by the time we came to film it in front of the audience, we'd started to relax a bit. I remember we were shooting a scene which was an Ann Summers party hosted by Dorien. We had loads of female extras there for it and one of them said to us afterwards, 'You know what you've done here? You've got a huge hit on your hands, girls.'

So it wasn't just us who had the sense that this was the start of something which was going to be big. I thanked the woman and said I hoped so.

Over the next couple of months, the more we filmed, the more we loved it. The whole team was a dream to work with and the studio audiences were roaring with laughter, so we knew we were doing something right.

Then, with all six episodes in the can, we got word that the series was to launch on BBC One on Monday 16 October 1989, which is the day everything went mad and has been mad ever since.

Early birds

The first episode caused quite the stir. Me, Pauline and Lesley went to our producer Esta Charkham's house to watch it going out. We were all petrified because we didn't know how people were going to take it.

After it finished, Esta said she was going to ring and check whether anyone had phoned up the BBC to comment. These days you just have a look at Twitter and the rest of social media to see what people are saying, but at the time this was the quickest way to gauge the public reaction.

So she made the call and when she put the phone down, she told us that so far there had been a hundred complaints because Pauline had said the word 'bastard'. Apparently it was the first time a woman had said that word in a sitcom – in *Bread*, Grandad said it all the time and no one batted an eyelid. We started panicking that we were going to get pulled before the next episode even went out.

Esta said not to worry; she had a plan. So we poured ourselves another glass of wine and got to work. The four of us took it in turns to ring the BBC complaints line, disguising our voices each time, to say how amazing we thought the new comedy was.

'That *Birds of a Feather* show? It's brilliant! And the three actresses in it were fantastic!'

I gave my sisters' names as contacts and the BBC phone must have been red hot with loads of people calling to sing the show's praises.

We thought we were geniuses coming up with that, although it backfired a bit the next day when my sister let the cat out the bag.

There was a very popular BBC daytime show called *Open Air*, which Gloria Hunniford presented, and they used to get members of the public on the phone to talk about the previous night's telly. They just so happened to give my sister a ring because I'd left her details when I'd called up.

This was live on the TV and Gloria said to her, 'We heard you really enjoyed the show last night!'

And Tina, putting her foot right in it, went, 'Course I did, my sister's in it!'

Carry on corpsing

Obviously we didn't get cancelled because it was a huge success, and overnight I went from being a little bit known to properly famous. I think the publicity we got from the swearing controversy ended up working in our favour, because even more people tuned in the following week. They loved it. And they still love it. I get stopped in the street all the time by people saying how much they miss it and how they don't really make comedy like that any more, which I think is a shame.

It was like going to work with your mates every week. We had the same crew from day one onwards – same cameramen, same make-up, same wardrobe – and we'd always make sure that they all featured in the background somewhere on every Christmas special. That was our little thing.

If we were ever filming outside London, we insisted that whichever hotel me, Pauline and Lesley were staying in, the crew did too. We wouldn't stand for us being put in a nice one and them staying in a s*** one up the road. And because it had such a family atmosphere on set, whoever came on as a guest star was always made to feel really welcome. I was proud of that.

The only problem in those early days was stopping us from laughing when we shouldn't have been. Once any one of the three of us went, it was nigh on impossible to bring us back again and we'd be helpless while the poor director was tearing his hair out. We were terrible for the corpsing.

I remember one scene where I was supposed to be lying in bed with Pauline when the doorbell rings. My line was: 'I wonder who that is.' Only the doorbell didn't ring until after I'd delivered the line and the audience started laughing at that little mishap. That set me and Pauline off and we literally could not stop. We were almost ordered off set to calm down, because obviously wasting time like that in a studio costs a lot of money.

Another time Pauline had to put the phone down, turn to me and say, 'It's Chris. He's got testicular cancer.' So, you know, a really serious line. But we could not stop laughing to the point where it was physically painful. I'd look at her and say, 'It ain't f***ing funny, Pau!' and then we'd start off all over again. In the end we had to shoot the scene without making eye contact with each other; I think I had to stare at the wall because it was hopeless otherwise.

We had a director called Nic Phillips who introduced a thing where he'd say 'Gordon Jackson!' (the actor who played the butler in *Upstairs, Downstairs*) whenever we corpsed to snap us back out of it. I've no idea why that started, but if we got the giggles Nic would shout 'Gordon Jackson!' and for a while it worked, but after that it would make us even worse.

'Suck a lemon face'

There were never any big arguments or anything like that, but there was sometimes a bit of tension and I'd usually be caught in the middle trying to keep the peace.

On a few occasions Lesley didn't have a lot to do in an episode, something she was never happy about and she made it known. I used to call it her 'suck a lemon face' and I'd have to give her a talking-to. I didn't know what she was huffing about really – if there was ever an episode where I didn't have much to do, I'd think that was great because I didn't have to learn many lines. Happy days!

I think it stemmed from the fact that Dorien started off as a character who played second fiddle to Sharon and Tracey. She needed us more than we needed her, but as the series went on the writers realized how good she was and Dorien became just as important. And the audience loved her. If I had a pound for every time someone has asked me for Dorien's phone number . . .

Party mad

We were a team who liked to party and there would often be a karaoke machine involved and fancy food like portions of chips in those little cones. As soon as we wrapped the episode we were filming that evening, the whole lot of us would head down to the bar at Teddington Studios and drink it dry. Eventually the poor bar staff got so fed up with our late-night partying that they left us a set of keys and the instruction to lock up on our way out at whatever unholy hour that was.

Once we broke into the executive producer Mick Pilsworth's office and tampered with his planning board on the wall and wrote *Mick Pilsworth is a bastard* on it. We stole the drink out of his cupboard as well – he always had a bottle of Famous Grouse whisky in there ready to pour for whoever he was sacking. We got into such trouble for that and had to apologize the next day.

When we rehearsed up at Elstree, we used to go for lunch at a local restaurant called Signor Baffi. Lesley could be outrageous when she wanted to be and one day she ended up taking all her clothes off in the middle of the restaurant. I turned away from her for one minute and the next thing I knew she was dancing around in her bra.

Lesley has never really drunk – she doesn't know how really. But she'd definitely had a couple of drinks that day.

I said, 'Les, where's your f***ing blouse?'

And she waved me away and replied, 'Oh, I was hot.'

As if stripping off was the only possible solution to that.

The royal seal of approval

We had millions tuning in for each episode, but I know there was a lot of snobbery about us. We'd get nominated for awards but never win. In fact, we would have to wait until 1999 before getting recognized when we finally won Best Sitcom at the TV Quick Awards.

We had a director called Tony Dow who had worked on *Only Fools and Horses*. When he came on to *Birds*, I think he felt like it was second best. We definitely got the impression that he didn't think we were anything like as good as *Fools*.

One of the actors from that seventies show *General Hospital* once said that we only appealed to the 'lowest common denominator'. I didn't even know what that meant at first but when I found out I thought it was a horrible thing to say. And it wasn't true either. We had fans from all walks of life and right across the spectrum. Lots of the royal family used to tune in. I've heard Prince Edward was a fan and Fergie too. Me and Pauline teamed up with her for an episode of our spin-off series *Jobs for the Girls* in 1995 and she still sends us Christmas cards every year. I really liked Fergie. She was slightly bonkers, a bit eccentric, but great company.

Lady Di used to watch. I met her a couple of times and she was lovely. Me and Lesley went down to Kensington Palace to lay flowers when she died and I'll always remember the stillness and the silence. It was eerie.

And Camilla Parker Bowles, now the Queen Consort, is another one who loved the show. When we came back for our second run in the 2010s, she came down on a visit to the studios and they asked her who she'd like to meet. She said she wanted to meet the cast of *Birds of a Feather*! We were chatting with her like you would a mate – she was talking about her grandchildren and you forgot that she was married to the future king of England.

After that me and Lesley got invited to a tea party at Buckingham Palace. There was a royal enclosure taped off from the rest of the event, but Camilla spotted us, came over and invited us in to join her. We felt a bit bad because Lesley's daughter, Lizzie, and Mark, who were our plus ones, were on the outside. But not so bad that we didn't stay there taking full advantage of rubbing shoulders with royalty for a couple of hours!

We were served tea in china cups and sandwiches with the crusts cut off, which I always think is a terrible waste, don't you?

I know *Birds* had a huge reach but I'm still constantly amazed at the people who know who I am. I bumped into Mark Rylance, one of our finest actors, at the premiere of his film *The Phantom of the Open* and he knew who I was!

He said, 'Oh, nice to meet you, Linda!'

I couldn't believe it. I can just picture him sitting at home watching *Birds of a Feather*!

I followed Gwendoline Christie into the toilets at a restaurant once. I love *Game of Thrones* and I was so excited to see her. I was actually with Lesley who didn't watch the show and had no idea who she was. Anyway, I spotted her nipping to the loo so I got up and went in shortly after her. I stood at the sink, making myself busy washing my hands and she came out of the cubicle but before I could say anything to her she said, 'Oh my God! I love *Birds of a Feather*!'

I told her I was a massive *Game of Thrones* fan and asked if she could get me in as an extra. I said I wouldn't even want paying, I just loved the shows so much. We had a bit of a chat and she gave me her phone number. I've never called her. Maybe if she'd spotted me first, she'd have been the one following *me* into the loo!

And just recently me and Lesley were on holiday in Majorca staying with three musical director friends – the West End boys as we call them. One of them said did we fancy going to lunch with Catherine Zeta Jones and Michael Douglas at their villa? He'd worked with Catherine on *Chicago* and they'd stayed friends.

I said, 'Do they have a pool?'

He said that, yes, they did.

So we got in this cab and headed to their place right up in the mountains, and Michael was waiting for us at the top.

'I'm so excited to meet the Birds of a Feather!' he said; obviously he'd been prepped by Catherine. He'd definitely done his homework before we arrived.

And then Catherine came out in her bikini and looking like an eighteen-year-old.

'Oh my God,' she said, 'I loved *Jobs for the Girls!*', which was a bit of a surprise.

Catherine and Michael were so nice to all their staff and knew their names, which I always think gives you the measure of people. It was the most beautiful villa you've ever seen complete with a helipad, and Catherine had done so much of the interiors herself. She'd done all the curtains and cushion covers.

We all sat down at this huge table for dinner cooked by their personal chef and the food was so well presented with pretty little decorative flowers on it – really posh. Me and Lesley were kicking each other under the table; we couldn't believe we were there! At one stage we went to the toilet together and I looked at her and said, 'F***ing hell!'

Bigger budgets

Birds of a Feather was sold all over the world and so we were recognized pretty much wherever we went. In the early nineties they tried to do an American version on the back of our success called *Stand by Your Man*, starring Rosie O'Donnell as the 'Sharon' character and Melissa Gilbert (she was Laura Ingalls in *Little House on the Prairie*) as 'Tracey'. It never took off and was cancelled after one season, and I wasn't really surprised. I'd heard the cast didn't gel that well and they'd all wanted the funny lines for themselves, whereas we'd swap lines quite happily all the time because none of us were bigger than the show itself. I'd say, 'Oh, that one's for you, Pau,' if I thought it would sound better coming from Sharon.

And we often did things on the hoof, so if something wasn't working or a line wasn't getting laughs, Laurence and Maurice would rewrite it on the floor while we were there and we'd always have input into that. Or we'd improvise something on the spot (my Anna Scher days serving me well!) and that would be worked into the script.

As the viewing figures grew, our producers were given bigger budgets to play with. In 1993 they flew us all out to LA to film the Christmas special – we always pulled out all the stops for our Christmas shows. The plot was that Sharon and Tracey had attended the funeral of their aunt Sylvie, where an old friend of hers had given them the key to a safety deposit box, which it turned out contained their real birth certificates.

They discovered that their father's name was George Hamilton and convinced themselves it was *the* George Hamilton, so they jetted off to Hollywood, along with Dorien, to track him down. That episode pulled in nearly twenty million viewers on Christmas Day, which is just mind-blowing – no show gets anything like that these days.

We had a ball out there. One night we went out for dinner where it was wall-to-wall Hollywood royalty. There was Sylvester Stallone on one table, Shirley MacLaine on another and we had to try and play it cool. I don't think we managed that to be honest.

A near-death experience

Money and success mean nothing if you've not got your health. I'd always been fit and well, so it was a horrible fright to find myself in hospital and at death's door before I hit forty.

A few years before, in 1994, I'd been admitted with gallstones while filming *Birds of a Feather* and *Jobs for the Girls* at the same time. Me being off work had thrown everything into disarray with two lots of crews having to be paid while nothing was getting done and it meant there was huge pressure from the insurance companies for me to get back on my feet and return to work as soon as possible. I probably should have had my gall bladder removed back then, which is the normal treatment for gallstones, but they couldn't afford for me to be out of action for that long and they needed me back filming. So they lasered them off and I returned to work forty-eight hours later.

That corner-cutting ended up nearly killing me three years later. It was October 1997 and I'd gone shopping on Oxford Street with my mum in search of costumes for the kids to go trick or treating in. I had a nasty twinge in my stomach which felt similar to the pain I'd experienced with the gallstones.

When I got back from that Halloween costume hunt on Oxford Street, I called my doctor about the pains and he said he would book me in for a scan and a blood test. But the twinges kept getting worse until the following evening when I collapsed with the most excruciating pain and was taken by ambulance to UCH.

I was right that it was to do with gallstones again, but this time they had caused a potentially fatal infection by penetrating my pancreas and I was diagnosed with pancreatitis. They gave me emergency treatment to stabilize me, but I then had to wait four weeks before I was strong enough for them to operate to remove my gall bladder.

I was so weak and frail, and Mark thought he was going to lose me. I thought I was going to die too, and I was scared witless. I suffered an anaphylactic shock one day when they were giving me morphine intravenously and they had to use the machine on my chest to bring me back round again.

For those four weeks I was nil by mouth and had feeding tubes inserted in my nose and throat, which was really traumatic. My mum and sisters would come and visit me every day and eat their big packed lunches off their knees right in front of me. Honestly, I could have killed them! 'Can't you go and eat that somewhere else?' I'd say to them.

On one occasion they managed to sneak our dog George in to see me, but it was a terrifying time and I was so scared when I finally went down for my operation, worried that I wouldn't wake up again.

I was in hospital for six weeks in the end, lost about

two stone in weight and even once I was back home it took a long time for me to fully recover. I've never been so frightened. A few months later, in March 1998, I turned forty and we had a big celebration to mark my milestone birthday, but also to toast the fact I'd survived.

I had 180 family and friends join me at a posh country club in north London where we danced to an ABBA tribute act and drank lots of champagne.

Pauline and Lesley were there obviously, as well as Paul Young and his wife Stacey, Su Pollard and Right Said Fred, who I'd got to know when we appeared in the video for their Comic Relief single 'Stick it Out' in 1993.

Later on, I went back to UCH to see the staff and thank them for saving my life. Because they used to inject the morphine into my bum so regularly, I stuck my arse round the corner and said, 'Remember this?!'

Dorien's finest hour

One of my favourite-ever episodes was 'Okey-Cokey-Karaoke' from series four in 1992 where Dorien performs 'Like a Virgin' while squeezed into a sequinned minidress. I know a lot of viewers loved that one too. Me and Pauline hadn't actually seen Lesley doing it until we arrived at the Hammersmith Palais where it was being filmed. And there she was, bumping and grinding against the singer David Grant before she lay on the floor, legs akimbo.

We couldn't believe it – the shocked reactions you see on camera were one hundred per cent genuine. There were loads of extras (not that you can call them that now – the politically correct term these days is 'walk-on artists') who were all gobsmacked too.

Ever the pro, Lesley did it in one take. We wanted her to do another one because it was so funny.

Do you know, she can still fit into that dress? What a woman!

Our fight for equal pay

Me, Pauline and Lesley always had each other's backs and we weren't afraid to stand our ground on the things that mattered. And this was never more evident than when we found out that we were getting screwed over with our wages.

We were all having a drink after work one night, when one of the accountants let it slip that over on *Only Fools and Horses*, David Jason and Nicholas Lyndhurst were getting paid double the amount we were per episode. We were pulling in just as many viewers on the same channel and working equally hard with long days from six in the morning until ten at night. The only difference was that we were women. We were fuming.

The three of us asked for a meeting with the TV production company we worked for, and we said we'd found out what the boys were getting and we couldn't see any reason why we shouldn't be getting the same. It was only fair. And we made it clear that we wouldn't carry on unless we got a pay rise.

We expected to have to put up a bit of a fight but to our surprise, that was all it took.

The producer said, 'You know what, I think you're right and I think you deserve it.'

And that was it. We got exactly what we'd come asking for.

We were really proud of ourselves for standing up for each other and sticking together, and it was another sign of what a team the three of us had become. When the three of us were together we felt indestructible.

Motherhood

First-time mum

Being a mum has meant more to me than anything else I've ever done in my life. I'd give everything back and would die a hundred times over for my kids.

I sailed through the pregnancy with Lauren and the birth was pretty textbook too. The early days of first-time motherhood in 1983, though, were far from that. I was expecting to be in this wonderful baby bubble like you see in the movies, but the reality was a million miles away from that.

The baby blues kicked in massively as I struggled to get breastfeeding going, and I spent the first few weeks with cabbage leaves on my boobs, which were in excruciating pain. Worse than childbirth, that was. The pain goes right through you and it's relentless.

I remember coming home from the hospital a few days after the birth and finding the flat in a right state, which really upset me. I liked things clean and tidy and I was angry with Tony for not keeping it nice during the time I'd been in UCH.

I just slumped down on the sofa thinking, *Oh no, what have I done?*

I didn't know how I was going to cope, how I was going to manage with this tiny baby who completely depended on me. It all felt so overwhelming.

We had this little shop over the road called Charlie's which I used to nip across to when we needed bread or milk. Now it dawned on me that I couldn't do that any more because if I needed to pop out, I'd have to take Lauren with me. I know that sounds like a really small thing, but it was like a symbol of something much bigger, and I'm sure a lot of mothers will recognize those feelings from the first few weeks. It wasn't about the corner shop as such, but more the loss of my independence and the realization that I'd never be able to do anything ever again without thinking about my baby. And I absolutely loved her! She was the best thing that had ever happened to me, but at the same time it was frightening to think that things were never going to go back to the way they were. This was my life now.

She just seemed to cry all the time; whatever I did it wasn't enough to stop her screaming, and I felt helpless and so frustrated. She'd been fed, changed, cleaned and cuddled – why the hell was she still crying?

When Lauren was about six weeks, I noticed she had cut two little teeth, which is really early to be teething but probably explained why she'd been so teary. It also explained why my nipples had been in such tatters with the breastfeeding.

My mum was great and always on hand to help. But it was actually my sister Tina who was the biggest support for me at that time. She had two children herself by then and knew the ropes, so she was able to give me lots of advice and reassurance, and I was so grateful for that. She had moved out to Essex with Sergio and I remember thinking she was so far away when I needed her, especially because I didn't drive at the time.

Tina helped me settle Lauren into a routine and once we'd got that nailed, things started to feel a bit easier. Unfortunately, just when I'd found my rhythm and was starting to enjoy being a mum, when Lauren was only a few months old, the nature of my job meant I had to go back to work.

Single motherhood

After Tony and me had split up, life as a single mum was far from easy. It was bloody hard a lot of the time – on top of trying to heal my broken heart, I had to piece myself back together while bringing Lauren up and keeping all the plates spinning with work.

But I was never going to be destitute. I had plenty of work and my career was in a healthy enough position for me to support myself financially while Tony chipped in with maintenance. After a while I told him I didn't need his money and I'd prefer he put it into a savings account for Lauren for when she was older. So that's what he did and when she was eighteen he gave her a lump sum.

It felt good that I was able to support myself and Lauren and we became a little team. I think those early years are part of the reason why we are so close today. As a toddler, she moved into my bed at night and slept there for the next several years, and it eventually took a therapist and an awful lot of star charts to get her back out again and into her own room.

I always wanted to be a mother. And I would have liked

to have had even more babies, but for various reasons that didn't happen. I like to think I've been a good mum. I'm always there for my kids and they know I'd do anything for them. My best times are when I'm with them. They've all got their own little ways, but I'm never happier than when I've got my kids (and now my grandkids) around me.

My boy

I found second-time motherhood much easier to get to grips with because I felt I knew what I was doing. Me and Mark had been married for two and a bit years when Louis came along on 20 January 1992.

Poor Louis had quite bad eczema, so we took him to a Chinese herbalist and also switched his formula to goat's milk, which did help a bit. But he had problems with his skin throughout his childhood and teens until he went vegan at the age of twenty-one and everything cleared up. His skin is absolutely perfect now.

Lauren hated him at first. She'd had me to herself for nine years and all of a sudden this little baby had come along and was eating up most of my attention. It also meant she finally had to go back to her own room after sleeping in my bed for so many years – Louis was in with me and Mark so there was no room for her, which did not go down well. Still, she grew to love him!

Louis is extremely private about his personal life and doesn't like me talking about him. I've got myself into trouble over that before, as you can probably imagine, but what I will say is that I'm so proud of the man he's become. He's so intelligent and articulate, he reads all the time and he knows so much about politics and what's going on in the world. He cares deeply about other humans, the environment and social justice.

He's very funny too. He sends me rude cards that crack me up. *Thank you for squeezing me out of your vagina* I got one Mother's Day.

I know I'm biased because I'm his mum, but he is an unbelievably talented musician. Mark bought a piano which I thought would just sit there gathering dust, but Louis started having lessons and really stuck at it. He has something special and I'm so happy he's making a living doing something he loves.

Losing my baby

It was 1994 and I was just over three months pregnant with what would have been my third baby when one day I started to feel really strange. It's hard to describe exactly what it was, but there was a definite shift and I knew something wasn't right.

Up until then, everything had been very normal, and when you've already had two, I think you get an intuition for these things. I called the hospital and they told me to come in for a scan.

Mark was out at work cleaning windows and there was no one else around to babysit Louis, so I had no choice but to take him along with me. I tried telling myself I was worrying over nothing and that everything would be fine, but there was a knot in the pit of my stomach that I couldn't shake. And as soon as they started the scan, I had an overwhelming sense that this was going to be bad.

The sonographer doing the scan went silent as she looked at the screen.

Then she said, 'Hold on a minute, I'm just going to get a doctor.'

I steeled myself for the worst, but my first thought was for Louis and how on earth I was going to hold it together with him there when they told me the news.

Luckily Mark turned up just as the doctor arrived back in the room and I've never felt more relieved to see him. He scooped Louis up and we waited as the doctor examined the scan on the screen.

After what felt like an eternity, he turned to me and said, 'I'm so sorry, but your baby has died.'

It confirmed what my instincts had already told me. I nodded, unable to speak.

In a way I think Mark took it worse and he kept asking why this had happened and if it was something we had done wrong. It was like he needed there to have been a reason for it happening. Of course there wasn't, and tests later told us that she would have been a girl but that she had had an extra chromosome and so would never have survived. It was just one of those things and no one was to blame.

They sent me home with my dead baby inside me and told me I was to come back the next day so they could carry out the procedure to remove her. I was stunned. This was my only experience of miscarriage and I had no idea that's what happened.

Going home knowing I was still carrying my poor baby was incredibly hard and both me and Mark cried our hearts out that night. It took us a long time to recover from the trauma and even now, nearly thirty years later, I still feel this heavy sadness when I think of her.

I think that is a pain all women who have experienced miscarriage bear for the rest of their lives. It's always there. I speak about it very rarely, but whenever I do, the tears always come and take me quite by surprise.

We called her Olivia and I often imagine how old she would be now and what she might have turned out like. But then I also wonder that maybe if she had been born, perhaps we wouldn't have gone on to have Bobbie Girl. Because despite losing Olivia, we still wanted another baby, and although I was wary about trying so soon after the miscarriage, by the autumn of 1995 I was pregnant again.

This time, thank God, everything went smoothly. I had regular scans to make sure all was well, and I'd feel this dread come over me at the start of each one, but our baby was strong and healthy and we were so grateful. The pregnancy also coincided with work being a bit quieter – *Birds of a Feather* took a two-year break between the sixth series in 1994 and the seventh – which I'm sure helped keep my stress levels down.

On 23 May 1996 I gave birth to Roberta Linda Lola, who we always just call Bobbie Girl. She felt extra precious to us, coming just sixteen months after we'd lost Olivia.

I'm so proud of the relationship all three of my kids have with each other, and good luck to anyone who says they're half-siblings just because Lauren has a different dad. They see themselves as full siblings – no halves about it.

The wild child

Lauren has always been the wildest of my kids and was forever getting into trouble (just like her mother, I admit). She went seriously off the rails at one point but it was her eating disorder which caused me the biggest headache.

As a kid, she'd been quite a big girl. Nothing major to worry about, but she didn't have the best diet and as a result she became a little chubby. Every Saturday, Tony would take her to the pictures where she'd get a big bag of pick 'n' mix, which didn't help, and she'd eat pizzas and pies at school for lunch, so the pounds piled on. But when her cousin Francesca lost a load of weight, Lauren thought she looked amazing and decided she wanted to be like that too, which is when it all started.

Over the next few months I noticed that she dropped a lot of weight, but as far as I could see, she'd not changed her diet at all. At first, I couldn't understand how she could be eating as normal but losing all this weight – it couldn't just be a growth spurt or losing the puppy fat. The only explanation was that she was bringing it all back up again. Lauren had bulimia.

I can't remember how I first discovered it, but it was more a gradual joining together of the dots. So it was the rapid weight loss, the fact that every time she'd eaten something she'd disappear to the toilet and then the secretiveness and defensiveness if we questioned what was going on. In the end, I confronted her and told her I knew what she was doing and was taking her to the doctor. She didn't deny it or put up a protest. There was no point because I'd made my feelings totally clear to her: she was my daughter, I loved her and we needed to get her some help.

Unfortunately the GP was no good and didn't take it very seriously. His attitude was: 'Oh, she's a young girl – she'll be fine. So she's a size eight? Don't worry about it.' He was completely dismissive and made me feel like I was worrying over nothing. But Lauren had never been a size eight in her life and you could tell she wasn't meant to be either, because she was all out of proportion with this lollipop head. To me she looked like a skeleton, and I hate looking at photos of her from that time.

Don't worry? Come off it. I was worried sick about her, and I didn't know where else to turn. Sometimes I'd follow her to the toilet and wait outside the door listening to see if I could hear her vomiting. But bulimics become really skilled in not making any noise when they're doing that and so she disguised it and I felt completely helpless.

I've never been one of those people to pass comment on my kids' weight or tell them they need to lose a few pounds, because my mum used to say that to me all the time and I know how it made me feel. Whenever we walked into a restaurant, she'd give me a nudge and say, 'Salad bar's over there, Linda.'

She had a thing about my neck as well, which has given me a lifelong paranoia about it. She would say, 'Ah, you looked lovely on the telly today . . . but, Jesus, your neck!'

I'd say, 'Mum, it's the only neck I've got! I can't do much about it!'

I hate my neck and wish I could have surgery to pull it all back, but I probably wouldn't ever have given it a second thought if my mum hadn't made such a big deal of it all the time.

Lauren had also started going out a lot and getting absolutely blind drunk, and I'd end up doing what my mum used to do with me, driving around, getting myself worked up into a state trying to find her to bring her home. Loads of things would be flashing through my mind about what might have happened to her. We talked to her over and over about how dangerous it was to get so legless and how she was putting her own safety at risk, but she wouldn't listen. Her dad, Tony, wasn't much help to be honest. Lauren could do no wrong in his eyes. I'd try and get him to support me in talking to her, but he would always take her side and say she was just young and having fun.

She was such hard work. Sometimes she'd be out all night and then go straight to work on no sleep. The worry about what might happen to her used to keep me awake at night. Thankfully she started to settle down when she met Steve. Lauren was working in a shoe shop in Chapel Market and one day Steve came in and they got chatting. We'd known his mum and dad, Brenda and Steve, for a long time and so we were really happy about it because they're a lovely family.

The relationship helped calm Lauren down and when she got pregnant with Lila, who was born in 2012, that's when the bulimia completely stopped. That was it – she knew she had to stay healthy for this little baby growing inside her, and Lila was so, so wanted because they'd taken two years to conceive her due to Lauren's endometriosis and other fertility issues.

I mentioned all that on *Loose Women* once and got into heaps of trouble for it (Baggy Mouth strikes again) but I don't think that's anything to be ashamed about. Nevertheless, I'd better stop there and zip it.

Turning her life around

Even though some of Lauren's behaviour over the years has nearly put me in an early grave, she has grown into the most wonderful woman and mother. She's like a combination of my mum and me and packs so much into her day. Lauren and the kids never have a spare minute. She's so organized as well. You know the kind of person who starts their Christmas shopping in January? That's Lauren.

She's worked since she was fifteen and so has always had her own money. She's been a PA for a fashion company, worked in a call centre, in a private nursery and then in a nursery for children with special needs. These days she works hard as a nanny and from what she put me through back in the day, she's turned her life around. Lauren is always the first person to go and help a friend in need; she's loving and generous and has always been fiercely protective of her family.

There was a woman called Jaci Stephen who used to write for the *Daily Mail*. Once she made some really pathetic comments about me and Pauline in the paper.

Jaci happened to be there at *An Audience with Ricky Martin*, which I went to with Lauren when she was about seventeen. I pointed her out to Lauren, saying, 'Oh, there's that Jaci woman from the *Mail* . . .'

I didn't think anything more of it until during the break a little bit later on when someone came up to me and said the Slater sisters from *EastEnders* had just had to drag Lauren off Jaci Stephen and that she'd been screaming, 'Don't you dare write lies about my mum!' What an image!

But she's always been like that, Lauren. If we're on holiday and someone tries to take my picture, she'll march straight up to them and say, 'Can you ask before taking a photo of my mum, please?'

The other two don't really take any notice, but Lauren is always on the lookout for people taking photos of me in my cozzie.

No trouble

Bobbie Girl has never given me a moment's bother. She's come out of her shell a bit more now but she was always really shy and quiet growing up. If we went to a restaurant in a big group, you'd find Bobbie under the table playing with her Barbies.

She struggled a bit at school because she was shortsighted and couldn't see the board the teacher was writing on. Mark had been dead against her getting glasses because he thought it would make her eyes deteriorate – that's what happened to him when he was younger. He's always had terrible eyesight and wore those bottle-bottom specs which he'd hated. So he was doing it for the right reasons but it meant that poor Bobbie was falling behind in her lessons.

Eventually Mark agreed that she couldn't go on like that and we got her glasses and her schoolwork picked up. I remember taking her to the theatre not long after she started wearing them and she couldn't believe she could see the actors' faces! She'd got so used to everyone looking blurry that she thought that was normal.

There were no unsuitable boyfriends or anything like that with Bobbie. She's been with her lovely partner Scott for eight years now, although she kept him very secret at first. She used to make him pull up his car in the turning opposite so we couldn't have a nose at him!

Bobbie Girl and Scott got engaged in 2023 and we are so excited for them.

Becoming Nanny Linda

I didn't think it was possible to feel the same love I have for my children for anyone else. But then I became a nan and it blew me away.

I'd been so excited when Lauren told me she was pregnant in the summer of 2011 and I was bursting to tell people. Lauren and Steve swore me to secrecy because they weren't going to tell his parents until they were back from a cruise.

Keeping my first grandchild a secret was going to be hard for me. And when I say hard, I mean completely impossible. I wanted to share it with the world! As I walked out the hospital doors to an empty corridor, I shouted, 'My daughter's having a baby!'

Then my phone rang and it was Lorraine Chase, who I've been mates with since the early eighties when we did *The Other 'Arf* together. I couldn't resist.

'Lorraine, I'm going to be a nan!'

So she was the first person I told. Over the next couple of weeks I told every taxi driver too.

The day Lauren gave birth in March 2012, the *Birds of a Feather* tour was starting a week-long stay in Wolverhampton so I only got to see Lila very briefly before having to leave for the Midlands. It killed me having to wait a week before I could meet her properly.

By then my mum was quite ill and she wasn't with us for much beyond the birth. I'm so pleased she got to meet Lila and the photos we have of them together are among my most treasured possessions – four generations of us, how amazing – but it was all tinged with such sadness, knowing she wasn't going to be around to watch her grow up.

Knowing Mum didn't have long left made baby Lila a ray of hope amid the despair. And when Betsy came along in 2016 I fell in love all over again. Being a nan is a gift.

My rival Nanny Brenda

If you watch *Loose Women*, you might have seen me talking about my arch-nemesis Nanny Brenda ... She's

Steve's mum, so the girls' paternal grandmother, and I'm constantly having to up my 'nan game' to make sure Lila and Betsy like me the best. Apparently her roast potatoes are better than mine and she bakes better cakes than me, so I've got some catching up to do!

We had her in the *Loose Women* audience once and they made a big thing about Nanny Brenda being there. She was asked what I did better than her and she said I was a better presenter, so she was really nice and took it all in good humour.

I'm only messing around, by the way. The competitiveness between both of us nans is a running joke and I don't mean it seriously. Brenda's a lovely woman and she's a good grandparent to the girls and all her grandkids – she's got loads of them!

Lila and Betsy

Lila is a worrier. Without meaning to Lauren has made her like that by giving the impression there's danger everywhere she goes. Betsy is the complete opposite. She is fearless and just gets on with everything without a care in the world. She has a lot more confidence than Lila. Betsy's an entertainer and will push her way to the front of the stage at a school performance, which is something Lila would never dream of doing.

Betsy is the most caring little girl and her teacher told Lauren just recently how kind she is with the other children in the school. She'll always look out for the ones who are on their own in the playground and she's particularly good with the kids who have additional needs, helping them and making sure they're all right. I cried when I heard that. I'm sure it's seeing Lauren working with children which has given her a good grasp of how to care for them, but I think it's also just in her nature.

They're both so well spoken – quite posh actually! I think they go to school with a lot of middle-class kids and that's sort of rubbed off on them. And they're obsessed with anything with a screen. Tablets, laptops, phones – honestly, they're like a pair of little addicts. Lauren has had to lay some ground rules and they're only allowed the iPad on the weekend now. It's banned Monday to Friday.

Lila loves her football and plays on a local team. I go to watch her whenever I can and she's a good little player, although she lacks the killer instinct. She's too nice and sweet. She won't run into anyone or tackle them in case she hurts them, so she stands back instead. Betsy wouldn't think twice about charging in.

They're two such different characters and I'm so proud of them both. I adore being a nan – I like it more than I ever did being a mum. I was working away so much back then and often felt pressured because of that. Now I have more time to be with them and I soak up every second – they're only a ten-minute walk away so we see each other almost every day. Lucky me.

Fame and (Mis)fortune

Perks of the job

I'm not going to lie, there are some really wonderful benefits to being famous. It opens doors which would have otherwise been slammed in my face. It comes in handy when you want a nice table in a booked-out restaurant and I love going to the big red-carpet events and the openings of West End shows. My grandchildren are so used to movie premieres that they think every time we go to the cinema there will be a goodie bag waiting for them.

I'm a people person, so I will always stop for a chat if someone recognizes me in the street, although I try to book holidays where I know the hotel is going to be full of Germans because none of them know who I am and I can go about the pool unnoticed.

I never really mind being asked for a selfie but I do have to draw the line in certain situations. Someone once put their head over the toilet wall when I was sitting having a wee and asked for my autograph. I told them to eff off and wait until I came out.

Buying my first home was a sign that things were pretty good financially, although it was Mark who was keen for us to get on the property ladder. I wasn't so sure because I'd always lived in rented accommodation and I was happy where I was.

I was scared by the prospect of a mortgage – my parents had never had one and it felt very alien to me. I said what if I don't work again and we can't pay it? But Mark convinced me that it was a good thing to do, and we bought a two-bedroom house on Arlington Avenue.

I didn't need to worry about not being able to meet the mortgage repayments. By the early nineties we were four series into *Birds of a Feather* and the ratings were higher than ever. Me and Pauline had also signed up to do the spin-off show called *Jobs for the Girls*, where each week we had to learn a new profession.

We did dog training, journalism, fishing and opera singing with Lesley Garrett where we had to perform 'Rule Britannia' live at Kenwood House in north London with a full symphony orchestra and in front of an audience of 9,000 people. What were we thinking agreeing to that?! We'd only rehearsed it as the two of us with a piano up to that point!

Pauline was pregnant with her son Charlie at the time and I promised her I'd sing her part if she dried. Well, she dried, and I just burst out laughing and started patting her on the back.

The Sarah Ferguson episode I mentioned earlier was a

Christmas special where we had to plan a fundraising party for her charity Children in Crisis.

Life could be really quite glam and we'd be doing loads of magazine shoots where they let you keep the clothes afterwards. That's a novelty which has never worn off.

Surfing the waves

There was a period during the nineties when we were having money thrown at us. Me and Pauline got signed up by Surf to do their TV commercials and also nabbed an Anchor Butter campaign, which saw us plastered across huge billboards – we were getting paid a fortune.

One time Surf flew us out first class to South Africa to film a new TV ad which had such high production values it was as if we were shooting a Hollywood movie. You know I told you about Richard Burton and his stand-in on the set of *Absolution*? We had stand-ins on the set of our Surf ads – a clear sign we'd hit the big time!

We were taken around in a stretch limo and I couldn't believe this was my life. I was also really embarrassed about being driven through the townships in this huge car, so I'd put my head down because it felt like we were taking the piss out of these people who had nothing.

The financial security we had meant that not long after Louis was born in 1992, me and Mark were able to move again, this time to a beautiful four-bed Georgian house with a sixty-foot garden on Devonia Road. The sort of house I'd never dreamed someone like me would own.

We did a lot of work to get it looking perfect and

I modelled the kitchen on Tracey's in *Birds of a Feather* with the big island in the middle. I had a cleaner and a gardener. We would host big parties for all our friends and I'd buy those fancy sandwich platters from Marks & Spencer, which I'd thought were far too expensive to justify a couple of years before. We took regular holidays abroad and our house was filled with beautiful furniture, lights which cost a fortune from Liberty's, and wallpaper and cushions by Designers Guild. Life seemed perfect and more stable and secure than it had ever felt before.

Giving something back

I've always tried to do whatever I can for charity because I know I've got this public platform and my career has afforded me a lot of benefits in life.

I was a trustee for Children with Cancer UK for thirty years and we raised over £230 million during that time. Eddie O'Gorman, who started the charity after losing his son to leukaemia and his daughter to breast cancer, has retired now, but I did everything I could for him and the charity and I'm really proud of the work we did.

I also did a lot with Plan International, who help children in some of the world's poorest communities. I sponsored a little girl called Rosa, who was the same age as Bobbie and lived in Bolivia, and the charity asked if I'd like to go over and meet her. So in 2003 I flew to Miami and got a small train to Bolivia, which I think is probably the longest journey I've ever made. I actually got strip-searched on the way back because Bolivia is one of the

Left to right: me, Debbie and Tina at Nanny Dardis' house around 1966. It must have been a Sunday because mum has dressed us in our best clothes.

The wonderful Anna Scher outside her theatre school on Barnsbury Square. I don't think I'm in this photo, but it's just how I remember that time – Anna surrounded by all us kids.

How happy do I look here? This was filming *Junket 89* in Dorset in 1970 and I'm pictured with my co-stars Mario Renzullo, John Blundell and Stephen Brassett.

Me as Maggie Moon filming the first series of *Shine on Harvey Moon* in 1981.

Me and my dad in his favourite pub, The Oxford in the late eighties. This was the pub he modelled our house on Elmore Street on when decorating it.

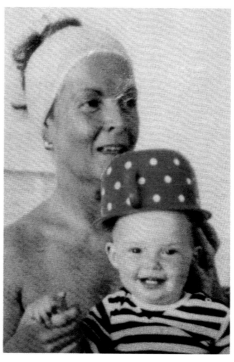

My mum and Lauren in 1984.

Me, Tony and Lauren on holiday in Majorca. I think this was about 1985 and can't have been much before we split for good.

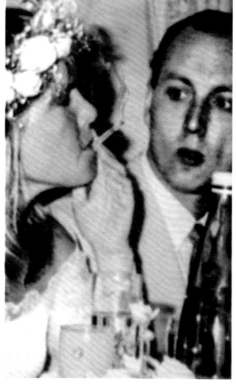

Mark and I on our wedding day in 1989.

Ahh! There's the three of us – me, Lesley and Pauline on the *Birds of a Feather* set. This would have been taken around 1992.

I love this picture. Me and Pauline filming series four of the show in 1992.

This was when we reprised *Shine On Harvey Moon* for a fifth series in 1995. Kenneth Cranham wasn't available to play Harvey so Nicky Henson took over the lead role and he's pictured here with me and Pauline.

My *Birds of a Feather* family! This is all the cast and crew together during series 7 in 1997. Lesley's in her dressing gown so I think we must have just finished filming. Maurice Gran is in the grey jacket on the right and Laurence Marks is in the checked jumper.

Me and Pauline in Florida Keys filming *Jobs for the Girls* in 1994.

The TV series *Holiday* asked me and Pauline to recreate Thelma and Louise's journey along Route 66 in 1993.

Rubbing shoulders with royalty! We did a panto in 1998 for the Duchess of York's charity and we got her on stage as part of the show. This is us post-show with Sarah and princesses Beatrice and Eugenie. And Lionel Blair who managed to jump into every picture!

Celebrating filming the 100th episode of *Birds of a Feather* in London in June 1998.

Me with Lauren, Louis and Bobbie Girl in early 1997. I think we were on a cruise here.

world's major production centres for the coca leaf and cocaine. Maybe I looked suspicious!

Meeting Rosa was a wonderful feeling. She was seven and I'd brought her a little make-up bag with the sorts of bits and bobs Bobbie Girl liked. She was quite shy with me at first but we made a lovely connection and it was heart-breaking seeing how little they had. They had nothing. This was poverty on a scale I'd never seen before. It was shocking.

After I flew back home, I wrote to Rosa and she'd reply so we had a little pen-pal thing going on, which went on for years. I'd tell her what my kids were doing and what we were all up to and I used to put dollars in the envelope to try and help out her family.

We did that for about five years until she eventually stopped replying. She'd be in her late twenties now and I do still think about her. I hope wherever she is and whatever she's doing, she's OK and that life is easier for her and her family than it was then.

The end of Birds

It was 1998 when we decided to call it a day on *Birds of a Feather*. It was one of the most difficult decisions I've ever had to make. Probably the most difficult, actually.

It was something me, Pauline and Lesley had been discussing between ourselves for a while, and the feeling was that, after nearly ten years at the top and more than ninety episodes, we needed a break. We wanted to try other things too. Pauline was keen to explore dramas and Lesley loved the theatre. I loved the show more than I could possibly say and it had changed my life and the lives of all my family, but I wanted to see what was out there for me beyond it.

We all agreed that this ninth series would be our last, at least for a while. None of us wanted to say goodbye to it for ever and we made that clear when we went to tell producer Mick Pilsworth the news.

'Maybe do one more, girls,' he said, trying to talk us round.

But our minds were made up and we stood firm. I think he knew we weren't going to be persuaded, although we didn't think for one minute it would be as long as sixteen years before we were back on air again.

We felt awful for the crew, though, because we knew our decision was going to put a lot of them out of work. And it was more than just a job. These people were our family and the thought of not seeing them every day was horrible.

Filming that final episode in the summer of 1998, I was an emotional wreck. I'm not sure how we did it without breaking down. At the end everyone burst into tears and started hugging each other. The audience must have thought we'd all lost the plot because at that point, we hadn't gone public with the news that it was ending.

If I'm honest, I wasn't completely sure we were doing the right thing and I'd had several wobbles worrying about that. We were walking away from one of the biggest shows on TV and extremely well-paid jobs, as well as some very special friendships. I worried that I'd never work again, but sometimes you have to take a leap of faith and trust that everything will sort itself out.

Losing it all

For several years I'd been spending like there was no tomorrow. But of course tomorrow did come. It always does. And it hit me (and my bank account) like a truck.

It had been all well and good splashing the cash and enjoying the finer things in life when *Birds of a Feather* was riding high in the ratings. And I could make hay while the sun shone when the big brands were paying us massive amounts to advertise their products and while our TV contracts were so generous. But when that came grinding to a halt, all at once my finances crashed. I had no regular work lined up to replace it and certainly nothing that was going to pay anything like as much as *Birds of a Feather* had. I found myself trapped in spiralling debt and I knew it was a mess entirely of my own making.

The wages and endorsement deals we'd been getting, I'd been burning through as soon as the money came in. I've never been any good with money unless it's spending it. I've always been very good at that! I had an accountant but hadn't ever bothered with a financial adviser. I actually can't remember taking any financial advice at all or ever considering making investments. I wouldn't have a clue where to start with that stuff. I just spent it.

Me and Pauline used to go and open places, like cinema complexes and shopping malls, for silly money. We opened the newly extended Brent Cross Shopping Centre in 1996 and each got paid several thousand pounds. There were so many people there to see us I felt like I was in

Take That! But all that cash just for opening a shopping centre? It was madness.

And I blew the lot.

It wasn't like I was out buying designer clothes or frivolous things for myself; my money was mostly spent on gifts for other people and taking them to nice places. We'd have luxurious holidays and fancy lunches in Harvey Nicks and Selfridges and it gave me great pleasure to do that for my sisters and my nieces and nephews, because we're a really close family. When the money was rolling in, I'd loved being in a position to treat the family or take my sisters and their kids over to Portugal, where I'd hire us all a villa. I'd taken my mum to Rome and also paid for everyone to go to Disneyland Paris.

I liked being in a position to help them out as well. I bought my sisters a clothes shop on Amwell Street, which we called Robbo's, and the two of them ran it together. Mark had owned the laundrette next door and when the shop premises came up, I decided to let Tina and Debbie give it a go. They did new clothes upstairs and second-hand ones downstairs, and they did OK for a few years. I also paid for my niece to go to private school for five years after she hadn't got a place at the school they wanted.

I dread to think of the amount of money I've spent on holidays over the years. I love going away and all the excitement of getting packed, arriving at the airport and then flying off to different places. We really did have the best times together, and the kids always say to me now what lovely childhood memories they have of all our adventures, so even though it ultimately got me into a mess, I can't say I regret doing any of that. You can't put a price on those experiences.

But the shopping had become like an addiction. I've got an addictive personality anyway and the shopping totally fed into that. I'd have massive sprees in HMV buying gifts for everyone and all the shop assistants knew me because I was always in there. I had store cards for every shop you could possibly think of – Marks & Spencer, Russell and Bromley, John Lewis – I used to accept every single one that was offered because it never felt like I was spending money when I used them.

And it was OK while the money was rolling in from *Birds of a Feather* but after that final episode everything just stopped. There were no more shopping centres to open. No more washing powder or butter campaigns. All those gigs dried up, and when you've been used to earning a lot of money and all of a sudden you haven't got any and there are no savings ringfenced either, that's quite frightening.

What I should have done was immediately get a handle on it. I should have stopped shopping like a madwoman and sat down and worked out exactly what was coming in and what we could afford. And yet I carried on spending as I always had. At the back of my mind I knew I had to rein it in, but I told myself it would be OK. I was kidding myself and inevitably started to slide into debt. American Express took their card back because you have to have a certain amount of money in the account for it to be usable. I think that was one of the wake-up moments where I thought, *Oh no . . . what are you doing, Linda?*

It got to the point where I'd be lying in bed at night

worrying about how the hell I was going to pay for this or that, how I was going to do nice things with the kids or help my sisters out. I just didn't have any money.

I didn't dare tell Mark how bad things were because I knew this was all on me and I was embarrassed and worried about how angry he'd be.

Whereas I'm hopeless with money, Pauline's always been so sensible with it. She likes nice things, but she's never been extravagant.

Eventually I had to confess to Mark. It was eating me up and I couldn't keep it to myself any longer. It turned out I had no need to worry about how he'd react – he was supportive and stayed really calm and said we would get it sorted together as a family just like we did everything else.

But I had to swear to him that I would stop spending. I promised to knock it on the head and I did. I only wish I'd told him sooner rather than worrying about it in silence. I should never have doubted him.

The first thing we did was cut up all the store cards and credit cards. I didn't need them and while I had them there would always be the temptation to spend. My accountant said I only needed a debit card and so that's the one I kept. We also came up with an idea of giving me an allowance, which was mine to spend on what I wanted, but once it was gone, that was it. So, to this day, I get given a set amount on a Monday and another one on a Friday, like pocket money. If I need more in between, I can ask for it from either Bobbie Girl or Lauren as they look after my accounts for me, but I very rarely do.

I don't have a credit card and this is the best way for me to manage things, because I doubt I'll ever be any good at budgeting. It's a simple way of helping me to live within my means.

I've been really, really rich and I've been really, really poor and I don't want to be either of them ever again. Being comfortable enough to look after my family and go on nice holidays suits me down to the ground. I don't wish for anything more than that.

Life after Birds

To recover from the debt I'd run up, and in order to get our finances back on track, I had to take some jobs I probably would have otherwise turned down. I didn't care about that, though; I couldn't afford to be choosy. I was determined to get us out of the financial mess I'd plunged us into and over the next few years I worked my arse off to do just that, accepting offers to go on game shows and talking-heads-type programmes which always paid quite well.

About a year after the end of *Birds of a Feather*, I was asked to go out to Australia for a production of Kay Mellor's play *A Passionate Woman*. It would mean a month over in Oz and the part would be alongside Geoffrey Hughes who played Onslow in *Keeping up Appearances*. It was a big job and a long way from home, but I thought it was a great opportunity, especially because if I was s***, it would be halfway round the world and no one would ever know. I couldn't lose, could I?

Geoff Hughes was lovely – he taught Louis to tie his shoelaces while we were out there, but his wife Sue didn't really seem to like children, which was unfortunate since I had all three of mine with me. I'd also taken Lauren's best mate Amy, who said she wanted to go back home more or less as soon as we'd landed in Brisbane.

Lauren and her are still best mates today and we do laugh about that now. As if I could have put her on a flight straight back to London again! She was fine in the end and Amy and Lauren looked after Louis and Bobbie while I was working.

They did a good job of that apart from the day they took them to a theme park and Lauren put Louis in this pretend guillotine and he thought he was being beheaded. He came back traumatized after that.

The night the show opened I was suddenly incredibly nervous. Just as I was about to go on stage for the first time I froze with fear, and I remember Geoff literally had to kick me up the arse to get me on. It went well in the end and thankfully I don't think I was s***. The reviews didn't say I was, anyway!

Julian Clary was out there at the time doing stand-up at the same theatre and he left me a note in my dressing room.

Dear Linda, it read. *It's nice to be in the same erection as you.*

Now, he'd upset Lesley a few years before by saying on *Room 101* that she would go to the opening of an envelope. So I wrote back: *Lesley Joseph's got a contract out on you, so keep an eye over your shoulder . . .*

It was a great trip all in all, and I took from it a lovely friendship with Geoff – I was invited on his *This is Your Life* a couple of years later. I remember him so fondly, especially his love of freebies. We did a load of radio promos for the show and Geoff would never come away empty-handed. Even if it was just a pen with the station logo on it, he was as happy as Larry. He was a great character and it was such a shame when he died in 2012 – sixty-eight is no age.

Just when things were looking up . . .

It seems that whenever life feels calm, there's a great big storm lurking just ahead of you.

I'd made a good recovery from the pancreatitis and apart from a brief flare-up in 2000, it hadn't given me any problems since the surgery to remove my gall bladder in 1997. By the early noughties everything seemed great both at work and at home.

In January 2003 I was at the Peacock Theatre watching *The Snowman* when suddenly I felt this crippling pain in my belly. I had to run outside to throw up in the street. Mark followed me out and found me collapsed on the pavement in agony. He managed to half carry me to the car and I was vomiting violently as he drove me to hospital, panicking the whole way there.

The doctors were amazing as usual and got the attack under control, but I ended up having to pull out of the rest of the panto dates I was doing and I also lost a job on a new sitcom I'd just started filming called *Odd Socks*, which was set in a laundrette. I was gutted.

Lynda Bellingham was drafted in to take my part and she couldn't have been more lovely about it, sending me a big bunch of flowers and a note wishing me all the best. She said that she was really sad that the reason she'd got this role was because I wasn't well.

As well as being upset about losing the work, I was also stressing that all this was going to make me uninsurable and that no one would want to hire me ever again. Thankfully that didn't prove to be the case and the pancreatitis has been managed well for several years now. I'm regularly monitored and it doesn't cause me any issues these days. Touch wood.

West End girl

I'd always wanted to be a West End star and so I was over the moon when a touring production of Nick Moran's *Telstar* I was in transferred to the New Ambassadors Theatre in London's Covent Garden in 2005. The play was based on the life of Joe Meek, the record producer and songwriter from the sixties who was gay and suffered a lot of abuse for his sexuality at the time. Joe was played by Con O'Neill, who is an absolutely brilliant actor, and I had jumped at the chance to work with him.

I played Violet Shenton who was Meek's landlady at his flat on Holloway Road. In 1967 he ended up murdering her and killing himself, and so my character was shot dead on stage by him every night.

As I was hit by the bullet, I had to stumble backwards and one of the boys would catch me as I fell. And I used to say to them, 'Make sure you pull my dress down so the audience can't see my knickers!' I didn't want to be flashing my underwear to all and sundry.

Once we opened in the West End in June 2005, we knew there were going to be famous names in the audience most nights and especially lots of people from the music industry, because that's what the show was about. I know George Michael and Holly Johnson came to see it and I suppose that added a little edge to things for the actors on stage and put a bit of extra pressure on. Anyway, because my character got killed in Act I, I used to spend the rest of the play sitting in my dressing room, chatting to people backstage and waiting for the curtain call when I'd go out and take my bow.

One night a member of the security team who I was friendly with popped his head round the door and said to me, 'There's someone really, really big in tonight.'

I said, 'I know there is – Christine and Neil Hamilton. Can't get any bigger than that!'

Ha! Little did I know.

'No, not them!' he said. 'It's Tom Hanks! He's sitting right there in the stalls.'

Thank God I hadn't known that before I'd gone on, I'd have been all over the place. Production didn't want the rest of the cast to know in case it put them off their stride, so I had to keep my baggy mouth zipped as they came on and off stage.

When the show was over, I went back to do the curtain call with the boys and as we were taking our bows, I whispered along the line, 'Tom Hanks is in. Pass it on.'

They were like, 'What?!' but having to hide their shock while they soaked up the standing ovation.

We all went back to the dressing room on a high when the doorman came in and said Tom Hanks wanted to come in and meet us. He was over in London filming *The Da Vinci Code* movie and had come to the show with his son. He'd brought wine with him, which was gratefully received by the cast, and he ended up staying for about an hour, just chatting away very easily, like he had all the time in the world.

He'd arrived at the theatre without any fanfare. Not like a certain well-known pop star, who had phoned the theatre in advance to request someone to escort her to her seat and made a right fuss about everything. There had been nothing like that with Tom, who had just walked in with his son and sat down like a normal person. He had a hat on so that people wouldn't recognize him, although I'm sure they did! He was just lovely and a real family man.

Mark used to pick me up every night, bundling Louis and Bobbie Girl into the car to come and get me. They should really have been in bed because it was past 10 p.m. and a school night, but they loved coming down at that time, it was like a little adventure for them. That night they came into the dressing room as well so there was me, Mark, Louis and Bobbie and Tom Hanks all sitting round together. Very surreal.

We talked about life and he said how much he'd enjoyed the show. He asked me what it was like getting shot every night.

'Oh, it ain't too bad, Tom,' I said. 'I'm only worried about flashing my f***ing knickers.'

The menopause strikes

I started the menopause during that run in *Telstar*. I remember that because I had to wear a wig every night, which made my hot flushes a hundred times worse. Those flushes were awful, like I was going to explode. They go through your whole body and there's nothing you can do about it except ride it out.

I don't remember my mum ever going through the menopause. I know she'd had a hysterectomy which must have brought it on. Maybe she breezed through it without a problem. Or perhaps she suffered with it but never let on to any of us. It wasn't something that was ever talked about regularly in the mainstream until fairly recently, thanks to women like Davina McCall, who has done some brilliant work to remove the stigma and open up the conversation.

The first person I ever met who talked about going through the menopause was June Brown. We were doing the BBC drama series *Play for Today* together in 1980, which was set in a department store, and I remember she spoke about it then. She would have been in her early fifties at the time and she was telling everyone how we all needed to know this for when we were older – the menopause 'dries everything up', she said, but HRT had been life-changing for her.

I loved June – she just said it straight. I was at a posh awards do with her once sitting at the same table when we all noticed she'd disappeared. We found her sitting under the table, hidden by the tablecloth, smoking a fag.

For me, my symptoms started quite early, when I was forty-four, although my sister was even younger than that at thirty-eight. I lost my sex drive and was tired and irritable, shouting at the kids all the time. Then the sweats started and, oh my God, I've never known anything like it. I was so exhausted and grumpy all the time, like I was

139

depressed, and I just wasn't myself. My hormones must have been all over the place.

Eventually I went to the doctor who prescribed me HRT and I've been on Climaval for twenty years now. I've since found out that lots of women have to fight to get HRT prescribed by their GP, so I feel really lucky that I was given it without having to kick up a fuss.

The relief was more or less instant and I felt back to myself within a couple of weeks. I came off it briefly when Tina was diagnosed with breast cancer in 2015 because it got me worried about the reported links between that and HRT, but after a fortnight the kids basically ordered me to go back on it. I was so awful without it! I'll probably be on it for the rest of my life because I'm unbearable to be around otherwise.

Grumpy Old Women

From *Telstar* I went straight into two of the most entertaining years of my career.

We started rehearsals for the live production of *Grumpy Old Women*, which was written by Judith Holder and Jenny Eclair, who is one of my favourite people to work with. There was me, Jenny and Dillie Keane in the show and we did a mini-tour in the autumn of 2005 before going on to do a forty-date sell-out national tour which finished with a four-week run at London's Lyric Theatre on Shaftesbury Avenue.

The tour was a riot. We would be in Oxford one night and up in Scotland the next, staying in hotels everywhere.

If the production company, Avalon, tried to put us up in rubbish places, we always had a plan for getting them to upgrade us.

We'd turn up at the hotel, I'd go in and suss it out, come out again and say, 'Nah, it's s***,' and then Jenny would phone up Avalon and put the blame on me.

She'd say, 'We can't stay here because Linda simply won't have it. You'll have to find us somewhere else.'

I didn't mind being the scapegoat – that sort of thing has never bothered me.

Jenny has such a good instinct for comedy and is a real perfectionist – she would be rewriting and editing the script all the time. She'd say, 'OK, that bit didn't get a laugh last night so we're going to put something else in instead.'

She was also brilliant at reacting to things in real time, like if a phone went off in the audience, she'd incorporate that into the show without missing a beat.

'Who's that?' she asked one night when a ringtone started up.

The woman whose phone it was replied, 'It's my husband ringing me.'

So Jenny took the phone from her and started talking to her husband on loudspeaker and it was hilarious.

She would improvise in the middle of the show to mix things up and keep us on our toes and I loved it. The show was phenomenally successful and such a privilege to be a part of.

Trip of a lifetime

The following year we took *Grumpy Old Women* to Australia for three months and I took Louis and Bobbie Girl with me. It meant taking them out of school, but I did that a few times over the years because I just felt these were once-in-a-lifetime opportunities for them, and the places they got to visit were just as important learning experiences as their maths and English. On top of that, I refuse to go away for several weeks without seeing my kids. As luck would have it, Louis's headmaster was Australian and he was all for it, so off we went. I took schoolwork with us and said I'd make sure they kept diaries of everything we did.

We went to Melbourne, Brisbane, Perth and Sydney, and it was really exciting for the kids. We were on Bondi Beach once when the lifeguards hit the shark alarm.

I went running down to the water where Louis and Bobbie were, shouting at them to get out of the sea. Loads of the Aussies stayed put in the ocean, which seemed mad to me, but maybe they're used to it and don't take much notice.

Both Louis and Bobbie were really picky eaters back then and would only eat chicken nuggets, chips and waffles. Bobbie Girl had to have ketchup on everything otherwise she wouldn't eat it and I'd carry those restaurant sachets around with me so it was always on hand for her. I'd just about given up with it but Jenny and Dillie told me they would sort them out and have them eating healthy stuff in no time. I think it was about a week before they quit trying.

'No, you're right, Linda. It's a lost cause.'

The kids adored Jenny and Dillie, and even asked me if they could get christened so they could be their godmothers.

Funnily enough Louis and Bobbie are now two of the healthiest eaters I know. They're both vegans and run marathons (Bobbie ran her first marathon when she was only sixteen!), so I always say don't fret too much if your kids are fussy about food because they'll figure it out for themselves in the end.

Top of the pops

I took part in some really bizarre shows around that time and I liked having the freedom to try other things.

I remember filming an episode for *The Bill*, which was a show I ended up guest-starring in several times over the years. I was playing a crack addict and to prepare I'd let my roots grow out and I didn't put on any make-up, expecting to be made up properly when I got there. I walked into the make-up room and they said, 'Oh, you're fine as you are.' Charming.

Then there was *Posh Swap*, which I did with Princess Diana's ex James Hewitt. He had to go to all the places that I would normally go, like Sainsbury's and Arthur's caff on Kingsland Road, which was known for years as London's best greasy spoon. And I visited his usual haunts like

Fortnum & Mason and did activities like clay pigeon shooting. We had to dress the part too. So they put prosthetics on our faces to disguise us, which were so good even my own family didn't know it was me. I looked like Mrs Doubtfire. But James Hewitt was a nice bloke and seemed game for anything.

Work-wise it felt like I'd turned a corner and I was getting plenty of interesting job offers coming in. I landed the role of Wanda Wise in the *Crossroads* revival where a young Freema Agyeman played my daughter. I'm so pleased to see how successful she's gone on to be.

I hooked up with Jenny Eclair again in 2010 when the Grumpy Old Women did *Let's Dance for Sport Relief* with Susie Blake and Lesley. We did a routine (of sorts) to 'Poker Face' and dressed up as different Lady Gagas. We had two weeks to learn it and Lesley, of course, mastered it after one day. The rest of us really struggled and I was a disaster. I just couldn't get it. I'd be counting, 'One, two, three, four' out loud as I was doing the steps and I kept on getting told to shut up by the others for putting them off.

So I stopped counting out and sort of grunted along to the beat instead, which they found even more irritating. No matter how much we rehearsed, me and Jenny just never got any better, but we had such a laugh doing it.

We got to the final but only because I spent £500 voting for us backstage on my phone! We were pipped to the title by Rufus Hound who deservedly won for his version of Cheryl Cole's 'Fight for This Love'. He was funny but he was also perfect with his timing and dance moves.

I've always been hopeless at dance routines and it's why I don't think I could ever do *Strictly Come Dancing* or

Dancing on Ice, and I've turned both of them down in the past. I did consider *Strictly* once but the kids told me I would be that year's joke contestant, which was charming of them but I knew they were right!

I'm not the world's best singer either. Although I have had a number-one hit single. In 2014 Gareth Malone put together an All Star Choir for that year's Children in Need to release a cover version of Avicii's 'Wake Me Up'. So there was me, Larry Lamb, Jo Brand, Mel Giedroyc, John Craven, Alison Steadman, loads of us. We went to Abbey Road to record it and it got to the top of the charts, beating Ed Sheeran and Cheryl Cole to the number-one slot!

I was actually really emotional when I heard it played on the radio and I didn't expect to feel like that. Mind, the kids pointed out that for our live performance on Children in Need, they couldn't hear me at all, and I think the producers had turned me and Jo Brand's mics off. Which was probably for the best.

Ben Kinsella

The night everything changed

I'll never forget the sound of Mark's voice as I picked up the phone. He was trying to keep calm but I could hear the tremble. His tone was deadly serious and I knew straight away that something terrible had happened.

'Listen to me,' he said. 'Louis is OK. But Ben's been stabbed.'

I felt my heart drop.

The murder of Ben Kinsella in the summer of 2008 had a profound effect on everyone who knew and loved him. It also shook the wider community in Islington, which I don't think has ever been the same since.

Ben was one of the loveliest boys you could wish to meet and he came from one of the nicest families too. He was a talented artist, a great cook and a straight A-star student. He and my son Louis were in the same big group of friends who had knocked about with each other since early childhood. Ben's older sister Brooke, who was famous for playing Kelly Taylor in *EastEnders* until 2004, was best friends with Lauren, and me and Mark were good mates with their parents Debbie and George. Whenever we had a do, we would always invite the Kinsellas over and we still do now because they will always be included in our family. And we will always have a special connection with them, however tragic that is.

It's extremely hard revisiting that night and the days, weeks and months that followed, but I can remember every detail as if it was yesterday. My memories are still so vivid all these years on that I don't think they will ever fade. It was 28 June and the kids had all finished their GCSEs and wanted to go out and celebrate at this bar called Shillibeers near the Caledonian Road.

While we gave our children freedom (unless they took the piss) we always tried to make their nights out as safe as we possibly could. Me or Mark would always drop them off in the car and pick them up at the end of the night and that's exactly what the arrangement was that evening. There were about ten of them, both girls and boys, who had grown up together and been mates for years, and they were so excited about their night out and the long summer ahead after months of studying and exams. From what I know, some of the group were mucking about a bit in the bar and there was an older boy who'd had a go at one of them for a so-called funny look he thought had been aimed at him.

One of the kids told this boy to leave the younger one he'd picked on alone – they were only young and out having fun; there was no need for any aggro. That was it. A stupid argument. No violence, no aggression. Just the sort of quick back and forth that happens in bars up and down the country every Saturday night and which no one gives a second thought to. But this boy wasn't going to let it go. He felt he'd been disrespected and went off and phoned two of his mates, telling them to meet him outside Shillibeers where they lay in wait for the kids.

They left the bar shortly before closing time at 2 a.m. and quickly sensed there was going to be trouble, becoming aware that they were being followed across the other side of the street by these three boys who were clearly spoiling for a fight.

It makes me catch my breath to think about how scared those poor kids must have been. They were only sixteen, and these three lads were older and bigger and had already boasted about carrying a knife.

The kids returned to Shillibeers and asked to be let back in because they were frightened about what was going to happen, but the bouncers said the place was shut and refused to open the gates which were locked at the front. We know from their later court testimonies that they were pleading to be allowed in, but it was no good, and I can't tell you how very, very angry I am about that. Those bouncers must have seen how frightened those kids were and yet they wouldn't help them. They left them outside like lambs to the slaughter.

Not knowing what else to do but get the hell out of there as quickly as possible, everyone just sort of dispersed, running down North Road as the three boys gave chase. Ben, who was the least likely person to be involved in a confrontation and hadn't been part of any of the friction that had occurred before, just happened to be at the back of the group, lagging behind, and so they were able to ambush him.

They cornered him between two cars before kicking him to the ground and then stabbing him eleven times in an attack which the court would later hear took just five seconds. He was crying out, 'I've done nothing wrong!' as they did it.

I can't imagine the brutality it must take to be able to do that to another human being. I don't think it mattered to them who it was they got, as long as they got someone.

The three of them then sped away in a getaway car and the CCTV footage shows the kids still running away as the vehicle flies past them. Ben appears on camera about a minute later, blood forming on the back of his shirt as he stumbles, disorientated, across the road.

The last sighting of him on that CCTV film is when he's met by Louis on the corner of North Road and then the two of them disappear out of shot on to York Way, which is where Ben collapsed to the ground. A passer-by called 999 and by the time Mark arrived on the scene a few minutes later, the police and the ambulance were already there.

He called me and told me what he knew and said I needed to get in touch with the Kinsellas as quickly as possible. Obviously I understood it was bad but I don't think it crossed my mind that Ben might die.

I tried to get hold of Brooke who had been doing a play in Dalston and had probably gone straight home to bed, exhausted. I tried and tried but she wasn't picking up. I didn't have the numbers of her sisters Jade and Georgia, and I knew Debbie and George were away at their caravan in Kent. Ben had been there all week with them but had come home for the night out.

I eventually made contact with Lauren – she was out

clubbing and pissed, but she sobered up pretty sharply when she heard what had happened.

'Lauren,' I said to her, 'you need to concentrate on what I'm saying because it's serious. You've got to get hold of Brooke and tell her Ben's been taken to hospital on Holloway Road. She needs to get there as soon as possible.'

Lauren managed to get in touch with Brooke via her sister Jade and the two girls dashed straight to the hospital. They'd called George and Debbie who'd got straight in the car and were on their way back to London.

Surgeons worked on Ben for several hours but it was no good. He was pronounced dead on 29 June shortly after 7 a.m.

Mark called me and I answered straight away – I was sitting up in bed waiting for an update.

I remember saying, 'Oh no, oh no, oh my God,' over and over. I couldn't believe it.

He'd been stabbed eleven times in the chest and back. He'd never stood a chance.

A community in grief

The next day we went round to the Kinsellas' house on Lonsdale Square. Debbie and George were obviously in bits and I felt so helpless because what can you say to people who have just lost their boy like that? The only thing we could do was rally round and be there for them, which we did and will continue to do for ever.

News of Ben's murder soon hit the papers. The fact he

was the brother of Brooke meant it got a lot of coverage and it felt like the whole country became swept up in this collective grief. And anger too. It completely rocked the local community in Islington. I think it changed everyone who lived there to varying degrees, and it went from being somewhere that kids all happily socialized together to a place where their parents were too frightened to let them out of their sight. A neighbourhood I'd always lived in, this sanctuary, my home, now felt dangerous, and there was this deep sorrow which hung in the air.

Two days after Ben's death, on Tuesday 1 July, hundreds of us walked through the streets of north London from Islington Town Hall to the spot on the corner of North Road and York Way where Ben had collapsed. It was dubbed the People's March and we wore white T-shirts and carried a huge banner with the words 'Why Ben?' written in red. All these years on, we don't have an answer to that question. I don't think we ever will because the whole thing is so senseless. Brooke and her sisters Jade and Georgia led the march and I was in awe of their strength. My heart broke for them.

It was the same at the funeral, which took place a few weeks later at St John's in Islington, and the Kinsella family were clearly devastated but stayed so strong, supporting each other. I'd been appearing in *The Vagina Monologues* in Cornwall so it was a long trip back to London, but I needed to be there. I got a light aircraft to Exeter and then caught a train to London, and I remember running through Paddington station to get a tube to Angel to try and get there on time.

The turnout was absolutely massive with over a

thousand people lining the streets. Everyone was wearing bright clothes just as the family had requested and lots of Ben's friends had these colourful wigs on, so everything was really vibrant and it was like a celebration of his life. But it was underpinned by this overwhelming sadness.

Ben's coffin was carried into the church to the song 'Ben' by Michael Jackson and Father Howard held the most beautiful service. Brooke did a reading, which was so, so brave of her. I don't know how she did it. The whole family has been so dignified throughout.

Charged, tried and convicted

The police had arrested and charged the three boys a few days after the killing and they were held on remand until the trial began at the Old Bailey in April 2009. It shocked me that the Kinsella family were seated in the public gallery so close to the friends and relatives of the three defendants.

I don't think it should be allowed, because it's already traumatic enough for the victim's family, and the atmosphere throughout the trial was charged and intimidating. It was atrocious. The tension was ramped up to the max and it was horrible, absolutely terrible. At times it had the sense of a war zone with the defendants' families on one side and the Kinsellas and their supporters on the other. God knows how Ben's amazing family kept their composure in the face of such provocation, but it felt like it was only a matter of time before someone exploded.

Over the course of seven weeks we heard the most

stomach-churning evidence as they all tried to pin the blame on each other.

When the jury found all three of them guilty, the courtroom descended into chaos. Some of their friends started shouting things out and one of Ben's cousins was spat at and the police had to step in to keep everyone apart.

Some people said our kids were underage and shouldn't have been in the bar anyway. So that means one of them deserved to die, does it? Teenagers have always gone into pubs and clubs underage. They weren't doing anything out of the ordinary. They were just kids being kids.

The Ben Kinsella Trust

The Kinsellas threw themselves into campaigning against knife crime and for tougher sentences for the perpetrators. They were determined that Ben would leave a legacy and soon set up the Ben Kinsella Trust, which has achieved so much through its work with young people, running knife crime prevention workshops in schools and supporting families affected by violence.

They met with politicians and managed to get the law changed to raise the mandatory life sentence for knife crime from fifteen years to twenty-five. The tireless, brave and award-winning work the trust has done in the years since Ben died is nothing short of incredible. They are the very best of people and have shown how much goodness there is in the world.

At times it feels like we're all fighting a losing battle, though. Knife crime in London has never been worse, and everywhere you go it feels like you see flowers laid down or some sort of memorial to a victim. Some of them really stick in your mind, especially those close to home. A dad of two kids who lived next door to my daughter was killed with a machete. And in 2015 there was a fifteen-year-old boy called Alan Cartwright who was murdered on Caledonian Road, not far from where Ben was stabbed, when an older boy tried to steal his bike. Such a sickening waste and just indescribably sad. There was a teenage boy stabbed to death in Highbury Fields, which is only up the road from us, and an incident on Essex Road where a female police officer tackled a suspected gang member who was armed with a machete. Every time it happens, it sends a chill down my spine and I'm transported back to that terrible night in 2008.

I don't know what the answers are, but shortly after Ben's murder *The One Show* sent me out to Chicago to do a report on how they were dealing with street violence there. I met former gang members who now work for outreach projects as 'peacemakers' and 'violence inter-rupters'. They told me how they used to be the problem but now they are the solution, and the strategy – alongside restorative justice programmes where criminals meet the families of victims – was working. Street violence was down by as much as seventy per cent in some of the areas they were targeting.

Whatever the solutions, they are too late for Ben. A few weeks after he died, George and Debbie received his GCSE results and they were all A*s and As. He was a boy with a big future ahead of him and it was all snatched away for no reason whatsoever.

We were all deeply affected by what happened and it triggered a lot of anxiety in me. I found it very difficult to leave the kids on their own or to think of them going anywhere alone. I lived on the edge, in constant fear of them being harmed; I needed to know where they were at all times.

We started taking Bobbie Girl to and from school every day to make sure she was safe. Even when she started at fashion college on Oxford Street after leaving school we'd drop her there and pick her up every day. Before this, if they didn't answer their phones, it would mildly aggravate me. Now it would cause a huge panic and I'd be convinced it meant something terrible had happened until they called me back. They learned to adapt to this and made sure they always answered when I called or phoned me straight back if they'd missed it. I just wanted to keep everyone safe and secure, but trying to control that as much as I could was exhausting and at times it felt impossible.

It wasn't a healthy way to live but I couldn't help it. My nerves were all over the place and I carried this dread and restlessness with me everywhere. I've never been able to let go of that, not completely. It's the same anxiety which would fester away and then flare up years later, making me extremely unwell and forcing me into the battle of my life. But there have been positives to focus on and never more so than on the fourteenth anniversary of Ben's death in 2022 when Brooke gave birth to her second child – a baby boy she named Ben.

I mean, what are the chances of that? Honestly, the fact he was born on that date was just extraordinary and it made me emotional on so many levels. When I heard the news, I started crying. I was so excited and thrilled for Brooke and for all her family. I couldn't be happier for them – to be given such a gift on the same date that they had lost so much is amazing.

I don't know if I believe in fate, but this certainly does feel like it was meant to be. After the most appalling tragedy, something really beautiful happened and baby Ben, Brooke's little miracle, is all the more precious because of that. And as Brooke has said, he is named after the very best of men.

Grief

Losing Dad

Grief often comes knocking when you least expect it. And it doesn't matter how many loved ones pass, the loss doesn't get any easier to bear.

Within days of Bobbie Girl being born in 1996, I got a phone call which would burst our baby bubble and blow our family apart. My dad's friend called to say he'd just been with him to see a Brian Conley show at the theatre and it had got him worried, because it was clear he was really struggling.

'Your dad looks terrible, Linda,' he said. 'He was having difficulty walking and breathing. I thought you'd better know.'

His friend had told him he needed to get checked out but, typically, my dad had played it down and said it was nothing and he'd be fine.

I gave my dad a ring and told him about the conversation I'd just had. He said it was true he'd had a bit of a chest infection which he couldn't seem to shake off. The GP kept prescribing him antibiotics which had failed to shift it, although he was sure it wasn't anything to worry about. Even so, I was concerned. I knew there was something not right – the fact it wasn't clearing up told me this was more than just a chest infection.

At the time my dad was running a pub called the Blue Anchor in Folkestone with his girlfriend Jenny, who we weren't too fond of. He'd always wanted a pub, but when he got one, he hated it. He used to say he'd just get sat down to watch the football on the telly when a barrel would need changing.

I told my dad to take a break from the pub and come with Jenny to stay at our place for a few days so they could get some rest, spend some time with the new baby and hopefully shake off the infection.

When he arrived at the house I was shocked at what I saw. His friend had been right – he couldn't walk without gasping for breath. He needed support to get up the stairs and could only come down them by sitting on his bum.

I told Dad I was going to ring Dr Forecast, who did the medicals for us on *Birds of a Feather*, and ask him to check him over. I really trusted Dr Forecast and I'd known him for years, so I knew my dad would be in good hands with him.

He told me to take him along the next day. As I'd only just had Bobbie Girl, it was my sister Tina who accompanied Dad to the surgery on Harley Street.

As soon as they left, Dr Forecast phoned me and said, 'I was hoping it was TB, but I'm sorry to say I think your dad has lung cancer.'

It shouldn't have come as a shock – after all, my dad had been smoking since he was ten years old and by this time was on about sixty fags a day. He was a proper chain-smoker, lighting another up as soon as the last one had finished, and he'd always had this cough. In fact, you'd hear that cough before you saw him.

The walls in his front room were yellow from him and Jenny chuffing away on these cigarettes. But it still floored me to hear the words 'lung cancer'.

It was the strangest mix of emotions to have my beautiful Bobbie Girl, who I loved with all my heart, and yet to see my dad so desperately ill. Everything is supposed to be wonderful when you have a baby, except it wasn't, and instead I was just all over the place because things deteriorated very rapidly after that.

My dad stayed over at my house that night, sleeping in the front room on the sofa with Jenny because he couldn't get up the stairs. The next day I was doing an 'at home' magazine shoot with Bobbie for *OK!* – I used to do things like that with the kids and put the money into a bank account for them for when they were older. But just as the camera crew turned up, my dad took a turn for the worse and we had to call an ambulance. He was blue-lighted to the Brompton Hospital in Chelsea with me, Tina and Debbie following behind. I had to take Bobbie Girl with me because I was breastfeeding and couldn't leave her. When we got there, my dad couldn't make eye contact with any of us. I think he knew then that this was it.

My memories of the next few days are hazy. They seemed to merge into one and I lost all concept of time. At one point they were going to amputate one of his legs, which he would have hated because he was a really vain man. But it didn't matter in the end because things were too far gone. All his veins collapsed and there was no coming back from that.

The four of us – me, Tina, Debbie and Jenny – were all with him when he went on 2 June 1996, but he died in the most terrible pain, which still tears me apart to think of. I try to block it from my mind but it has haunted me all these years.

It was eight days between that phone call from his friend to his death, so really quick. That's how bad he was. He was fifty-seven, which is far too soon to go, although it was only when I got to that age myself a few years back that I realized just how young he'd been to die.

The biggest loss

I took it really badly, all of us did. And my mum . . . God, she was completely devastated. Bereft. I told you before that she'd never stopped loving him, and I don't think she'd ever considered that he might die before her.

They'd had a good relationship, even though they'd not been a couple for more than twenty years by that stage. When Mum had her heart attack in 1989, my dad had been so good, coming round to visit her and doing whatever he could to help out. I'm glad that despite all the hurt and anger of the past, they'd managed to salvage a friendship, and I know it was really important to my mum.

Lauren, who was only thirteen at the time of Dad's death, was brilliant with everything. I was so proud of the way she helped me with Louis and Bobbie Girl while

I was struggling with grief and trying to organize the funeral. She'd put Louis's tea on and take Bobbie from me, telling me to go upstairs and have a lie-down.

I have a really close relationship with Bobbie Girl, as I do all my kids, but she's never been big on cuddling for some reason. Sometimes I wonder if it's to do with the fact she was born in the middle of that crisis and I was mourning my dad during those first few weeks of her life. I'm probably reading too much into that but it's something I've thought about.

There were a fair few people – women, if we're going to be specific about it – who turned up at the funeral that we'd never seen before. We had our suspicions that one of them might have been the woman he'd been with when he'd told us he was a night watchman, but we couldn't be sure, and it wouldn't have been right to go round asking. And we have a feeling there might have been a love child somewhere along the way, although again we couldn't have proved it. There was a woman my age who we knew Dad had been seeing because Mark's mum had caught him snogging her in one of the walk-ways on the estate she lives on. My sisters had been saying they would have a fit if she dared show up, but I told them not to turn the funeral into a slanging match and just to leave it. She did come along, but thankfully they took my advice and the day went calmly with my dad sent off to the strains of Frank Sinatra singing 'My Way', which I thought was rather fitting in the end.

We also played 'To All the Girls I've Loved Before' as a nod to his womanizing ways. Tina and Debbie said it was in bad taste, but I said it would lighten the mood a bit, as well as capturing some of the cheekiness my dad was known for.

My dad wasn't a bad person. He loved us and we loved him right back. I've still got his old leather jacket and a pair of his trousers and for years after he died I could smell him. Secret Service cigarettes. It was always cigarettes.

Life without him was so hard. He'd been such a big character, so he was always going to leave a huge void in our family. I was closer to my dad than my mum because we shared a sense of humour and I didn't know what I was going to do without him. I felt so lost. But I also felt that I couldn't mourn properly because I had a new baby to look after as well as Lauren and Louis. Although maybe having those distractions helped me through it and took my mind off the grief.

I missed him dreadfully. I still miss him now all these years later.

Anti-smoking family

My dad's death has definitely affected the way my family views cigarettes. Lauren and Bobbie Girl are fiercely anti-smoking because of it. Mark as well, because he's a real health freak. Lauren won't even touch a packet of cigarettes she's so disgusted by them. She point-blank refuses to buy them for anyone.

I come from a family of smokers on both sides and it was so normal to me growing up. I smoked all through my pregnancy with Lauren, but that was in the early eighties when we really didn't know how damaging it could be for the unborn baby. When I found out I was expecting Louis in 1991, I knew I had to quit and so I signed up to the Allen Carr Easy Way to Stop Smoking programme. I went to the first session and then headed straight to *Birds of a Feather* rehearsals, and I remember Pauline, who was more of a social smoker, saying to me, 'You're never going to get through the day without having a fag.'

But I was determined and I did get through that first day, then the second and it went on and on and I just stopped. I didn't have another fag for eighteen years until my birthday night out when all the family went to a pizza place for dinner. Lesley and Pauline were there too.

Tina and Debbie, who both smoked, went out for a fag and I joined them and ended up having a puff.

The kids spotted me and said, 'Oh, Mummy, you look really stupid!' so I put it out. But within about a week I'd bought a packet of fags and that was it – I was smoking in secret. I was mad with myself for starting again.

I'd take our Staffie George out for a walk and use that time to have a couple of sly cigarettes. One day I was on my way back with a fag in my hand when I saw Bobbie Girl and Mark coming towards me and I panicked and put it, still lit, in my pocket.

We stopped to have a quick chat when Bobbie Girl said, 'Um, Mum, something's on fire.'

The smoke was billowing out of my jacket pocket. The cat was out of the bag and I had to confess.

Another time Lauren caught me smoking in our garage downstairs.

'Mum, have you been smoking?'

'Er, no, no . . .'

'Yes, you have. I can smell it.'

The only thing I could think of to say was, 'It wasn't me!' Like I was some naughty teenager.

These days I have one every now and again – I nip out of the *Loose Women* studios for the odd puff with Coleen Nolan from time to time – and the kids know that, but I carry my nicotine inhaler all the time and that helps fend off a lot of the cravings. What happened to my dad is always on my mind so I know I should steer clear of the fags. If I started smoking twenty fags a day again, then they'd be traumatized and Lauren probably wouldn't even speak to me.

The British Lung Foundation got in touch shortly after my dad died and asked me to do some work for them, which I was more than happy to help them with. I supported a number of campaigns over the years and in 2015 we managed to get the law changed, making it illegal for adults to smoke in cars where there are children on board. I did an advert for part of that campaign and it's something I'm really proud of because that legislation has literally saved kids' lives.

Mum's dementia

While my dad had died young, my mum soldiered on. She seemed invincible.

Reet Petite, my beautiful, kind, straight-talking mum was the backbone of our family and the strongest woman

I knew. And so watching her go from being so strong, fit and healthy to this shadow of a woman weighing just five stone and having to be hoisted in and out of a hospice bed was gut-wrenching.

At first we'd thought she was depressed. My stepdad Johnny had died of prostate cancer two days before Christmas in 2010 after we had all helped nurse him through his final months. Mum seemed really lost without Johnny, but we soon realized there was more to her strange mood than just grief and feeling down, because the behaviour got increasingly erratic.

We'd be shopping with her at Chapel Market and she would just wander off without warning and we'd lose her. Luckily everyone down there knew her so we'd just go, 'Anyone seen our mum?' and someone would say which direction she'd headed off in.

We got her a mobile phone which we showed her how to use but it was just a waste of time really. I don't think she could even hear it ringing. Sometimes she would ask a stranger to call one of us to find out where we were. 'We're looking for you, Mum!' we'd say, trying not to get exasperated with her.

She needed the toilet all the time and was having problems with incontinence, and she'd also started smoking again, forgetting that she'd quit years before. I caught her on the doorstep having a fag once and she tried to make an excuse to cover it up, but it was really worrying.

I was round at hers one evening when the lights went out and the trip switch needed flipping on again, so I climbed up a chair to do it but fell off with a huge clatter and really hurt myself.

I was calling for her. 'Mum! Can you come and help me up?'

And she shouted back, 'I'm watching *CSI*!'

Admittedly she had always loved her *CSI*, but I was injured and normally she'd have been there like a shot. It was like she was on another planet a lot of the time.

Some nights she'd come over to my house at 9 p.m., smartly dressed and all made up, to let me know she was going to Sainsbury's and to ask if I wanted anything.

'It's nine o'clock at night, Mum,' I'd say. 'What are you doing?'

All these little things which were just so out of character started to build up.

When you see someone every day it's often hard to recognize the extent of the decline because it's happening bit by bit. But when we all went over to Ireland for my uncle Paddy's wedding anniversary the wider family who hadn't seen her for a while really noticed the weirdness. Everyone was asking me what the matter was with my mum. She was quite vacant and struggled to remember a lot of things, including people's names, and I had to help her to go to bed early and get her undressed, which was not normal.

She'd look in the mirror and go, 'Jesus! Look at the state of me. I look terrible!' when she looked absolutely lovely and the same as she always had done. But it was when she started stripping off that we knew we needed to get her help. She would undress in front of my nephews, changing into her nightdress and putting her clothes on the radiators, and we've definitely never been the sort of family that sees each other naked.

The family took her to see the *Birds of a Feather* tour at the Southend Cliffs Pavilion in March 2012 – there was Tina, Debbie, Bobbie, who would have been about sixteen, and my mum sat together in the theatre. It was also my birthday, so it was a special occasion, and they were all really looking forward to the show and a night out together. But all of a sudden my mum started removing her clothes. She took her jacket off and her boots and then she did the same with her socks and put them on the shoulder of the man in front of her.

Bobbie was horrified. 'Nanny's undressing!' she said as my sisters hurriedly took the socks off the poor bloke's shoulder and told my mum to put them back on again.

After the show, me, Pauline and Lesley took everyone out for an Italian and that was the last night out we ever had with my mum. You could tell she wasn't right.

We got her a referral to a specialist who confirmed dementia, and although she was still living at home she went downhill so quickly that she wouldn't stay there for long.

The beginning of the end

As you know, she was a bit of a show-off, my mum. When my nephew Tom started seeing a girl who had a lovely big house, she'd tell people, 'Tom's girlfriend has a house with a swimming pool, you know.' So when I'd bought a flat on Elmore Street, just a few doors away from the house she'd brought us up in, she loved to tell everyone, 'Of course I own my own house now.' That's where she was living as she started to deteriorate. One of us made sure we stayed with her every night and for a few weeks that arrangement worked OK. But dementia is such a cruel illness. You just lose them and there's no hope of recovery because there's no cure. The only guarantee is that they're going to get worse.

Mum had lost all her appetite and was wasting away before our eyes. To try and build her up, we used to stock her fridge with her favourite McDonald's milkshakes, which are loaded with calories, but she even stopped having them.

One of the community nurses who came to visit her suggested she go to the Marie Curie Hospice in Hampstead for a week's respite, but she ended up there for four months and never came home again.

She suffered a series of urinary tract infections while she was there, which sent her a bit delirious, and the doctors were also worried about a lump in her stomach. They diagnosed her with stomach cancer, which explained the weight loss, and we knew then that it was only a matter of time before we lost her.

One of us went down to Marie Curie every day and she got the best treatment ever there. They were amazing, they really were, and they looked after us as well. And I don't think my mum was the easiest patient. She got to the point where she'd say out loud anything that popped into her head. If she saw a larger person in the hospice, she'd go, 'Jesus! Look at the size of that!'

We'd go, 'Mum! You can't say that!' but it didn't make any difference by that stage.

She was too frail to have any treatment for the cancer

and so in her final weeks we made the decision to put her on the Liverpool Care Pathway, which was a scheme for end-of-life care they used back then to give dying patients dignity.

She slips away

You know people often talk about having a beautiful birth? Well, my mum had a beautiful death. It came on 22 August 2012 and she was surrounded by me, Tina, Debbie and my cousin Jackie, who she was really close to.

We'd all gone to sleep on mattresses on the floor and the nurse said later that when it's quiet that's when they slip away a lot of the time.

I woke up with the nurse saying, 'She's gone, Linda.'

'Gone where?' I asked because I was still half asleep.

And then I knew. That was it.

She'd died very peacefully in a room with people who loved her, and that's all you can hope for in death, isn't it?

We all started crying because although we knew it was going to happen it's still heartbreakingly sad when it does. She was only seventy-five, so not old in today's terms really.

My mum had known exactly the funeral she wanted and had planned it to the last detail, saving for years to pay for it all. She was taken from her flat on Elmore Street to Our Lady and St Joseph's on Balls Pond Road – just a five-minute journey – by horse and carriage in the most beautiful coffin.

We'd had a wake where everyone came to sit around

the open casket, but I didn't go because I didn't want to see her like that. Tina was amazing and she did Mum's hair and make-up just how she liked it, so she looked as pristine and perfect as always.

She had all her own teeth, right to the end, apart from one which she used to take out in restaurants and wrap up in a napkin before she ate. I'd always tell her not to do that because on at least two occasions we'd ended up rooting through the rubbish bins after the waiting staff had cleared the table and inadvertently taken my mum's tooth away with them.

The family from Ireland came over for the funeral and we gave her a really good send-off and I hope we did her proud. She's buried next to my dad in the cemetery at Finchley, which is what they would have both wanted. My dad's marble headstone is slightly bigger and my mum wouldn't have liked that, so we got them a bench as well with both their names on. Hopefully that'll keep her happy.

On the other side of my dad is a woman called Doris Pratt and we always imagine him saying, 'What'd you put me next to that Pratt for?'

The final months had been draining for all of us. We definitely couldn't have managed the situation by keeping her at home. I always say to the kids that if I ever get dementia, put me in a home. Don't even question it. I don't want them to have the burden of looking after me. But I'd do it all again in a heartbeat. She was the best mum and nanny and I miss her every day.

Me with my sisters: Tina on the left and Debbie in the middle. This was at my nephew's wedding in La Manga in 2015. Tina is wearing a headscarf because she was having treatment for breast cancer.

This is Rosa, a little girl in Bolivia who I sponsored through the charity Plan International. I flew out to meet her in 2003 and she was very shy but so lovely. We wrote to each other for years and I'd always put a few dollars in the envelope.

On stage in *Telstar* with Con O'Neill in the West End in 2005.

Me, Jenny Eclair and Dillie Keane with our best *Grumpy Old Women* faces on in 2006.

Chatting to Camilla Parker Bowles, our now Queen Consort, about our grandkids during her visit to the ITV studios in 2015. Apparently she specifically requested to meet us!

Here we are ahead of the *Birds of a Feather* stage show in 2012.

At boot camp in Ibiza with Nadia, Saira, Andrea and our lovely make-up girls in 2018.

Saira, Nadia, Andrea and me in Ibiza, 2018.

This was me and Nadia at Hyde Park where we'd gone to see Stevie Wonder in 2016. We kept on getting recognized and asked for selfies so we ended up hiding under a big blanket!

With my Loose ladies, Andrea, Nadia and Kaye. I think this was around 2017 but I'm not sure what we were filming!

Jane, Nadia and I having some Dutch courage in the pub ahead of our Body Stories shoot in 2017.

Obligatory lift selfie on our way to the NTAs in 2017.

Christine Lampard, Saira Khan, me, Stacey Solomon and Jane Moore at my sixtieth birthday in 2018.

Jane Moore, Denise Welch, me and Charlene White on the *Loose Women Live* tour. I think this was backstage at Newcastle. What a giggle we had out on the road together – I'd love to do it again!

Above: Doing the backstage thrust before we headed out on stage! We used to do this before filming *Birds of a Feather* and I was chuffed to be able to carry on the tradition with the Loose team.

Above: Kelly Holmes, me, Kaye Adams and Denise Welch all glammed up and ready to go out in front of the *Loose Women Live* audience.

Green goddess Janet Street-Porter, Kaye Adams, me and Brenda Edwards waiting in the wings. I think I did the most *Loose Women Live* shows of everyone. I wish I could have done them all!

Lauren, Louis, Bobbie Girl and me on holiday in a very rainy Paris in 2023. I'm never happier than when I have all my kids with me.

Lila and Betsy love looking for fairy houses in the trees around where we live! Here they are with their latest discovery.

I love taking Betsy and Lila to events – it's a lovely perk of what I do. This is us at the launch of *Trolls* on NOW TV in 2017.

Friends and Family

My band of women

The unwavering friendship of some wonderful women has seen me through thick and thin. Many of my mates have been by my side for as long as I can remember. Others have come into my life more recently but I couldn't now imagine it without them.

I think I'm a good friend. I'm loyal and steadfast and I'm honest. If anyone ever wants my advice or opinion on something, I'll be truthful, even if it's not what they want to hear. I only tell them if they've asked me, mind – I would never take it on myself to go up to someone and start dishing out unsolicited advice. But if they want my take on something, I'll give it to them straight, and I want them to be straight with me in return.

As well as honesty, my friends need to have a good sense of humour and understand that my own can be a bit strange. I laugh at inappropriate moments like if someone falls over or, worse still, at a funeral. I'm terrible for that. I don't know why but something comes over me and I can't help it.

I don't like people who are needy. You know, the type that gets all huffy if you've got other stuff on and take offence that you can't meet up? Can't be doing with that. My family will always come first and my friends know that.

The last (but not least) requirement I have for my friends is that they're clean. That's not too much to ask, is it?

There's something very powerful about female friendship. We've got a lot of shared experiences and we've all got the same hormones flying around so there's a lot of solidarity in that. I couldn't do without my mates. Some of them have even saved my life.

Pauline Quirke

As you know, Pauline and me have been mates since we were ten and there is literally nothing we don't know about each other. We don't see as much of each other as we used to but she will always be one of my most valued friends.

Pauline is a tough cookie and doesn't really suffer fools. Never has! She's not keen on being stopped for photographs because she's quite a shy person and doesn't go in for all the celebrity or fame stuff. She's just a very private person and likes to live a quiet life – she'd never dream of going on the reality shows or game shows that me and Lesley do.

Pauline hates live telly. She absolutely detests it! She doesn't have the confidence and she doesn't like anything where she has to be herself.

I remember going on the chat show *Wogan* with her to talk about *Birds* and I can't tell you what she put herself through before that interview. Terry Wogan was lovely and came to see us beforehand, but it didn't do anything to settle Pauline down.

To be fair, I was also scared stiff. It was the first time

we'd done a chat show and we'd got ready at mine, putting our make-up on and doing our hair and having quite a nice time. And then we go to the studio and absolutely s*** ourselves.

She's always been sick with fear at performing live too. We shared a dressing room at Elstree and on the days we were filming in front of an audience she would vomit in the sink before we went out to face them.

The first time we did panto, in 1991, the nerves would get the better of her every night, and she swore blind she was never putting herself through the hell of doing live theatre again. And she never did, until twenty years later when we took the stage adaptation of *Birds of a Feather* on tour.

I was heavily pregnant with Louis during that run of *Dick Whittington* at the Hackney Empire and was supposed to have been playing Alice Fitzwarren, which was the glamorous part. But because I was eight months gone and about to drop by that point, I ended up being recast as the fairy.

The line that got the biggest laugh every night was when I had to say, my big pregnant belly on full display, 'Five miles to London and still no sign of Dick!'

Our dressing room at Hackney was on the ground floor and the nearest loo was on the third, which wasn't great for a pregnant woman. We ended up getting a bucket and using that. The glamour!

Lesley was over at the Richmond Theatre that year with the most beautiful dressing room and en suite. And probably staff to feed her grapes and massage her feet, knowing her.

Lesley Joseph

Lesley is one of the most impressive women I've ever known. We row and we bicker like nobody's business but it's always in good humour and we can make each other laugh until the tears are rolling down our cheeks.

She tells me off for swearing so much. 'Linda!' she says. 'Your mother would kill you if she could hear you now!'

I don't think I've ever heard Lesley swear, come to think of it.

I'm sure she had some reservations about me and Pauline at first, wondering how she was going to fit into this friendship that went back decades. But she just slotted in and there was never any trouble between us. Well, nothing to write home about anyway!

We became such great mates over the years and our families did too – we've all been through so much together. I used to go and see Lesley's mum Vicki, an old-school Jewish lady who lived to 103. She was the most incredible woman and was still line dancing and playing tennis up until she was about ninety. That's exactly what Lesley will be like.

She's got the same figure she always had when we were starting out and she doesn't have a scrap of cellulite either. She walks everywhere. If I'm meeting her in the West End, Lesley will walk the five or six miles from Wandsworth to get there rather than driving or getting a taxi. And I say walk but Lesley marches. Most people would struggle to keep up with her!

Her house is fabulous, just like her. She's got a room that's practically a ballroom and she's collected china frogs for years so there are loads of them everywhere. Pauline collected pigs and I collected fat ladies like the ones from the Beryl Cook paintings, so we each had our 'thing'.

Lesley has always had very particular tastes and she isn't afraid to make it known if something isn't to her satisfaction. She once switched Harley Street hospitals because she didn't like the food in the first one. She cracks me up.

I'll tell you a story which sums her up in a nutshell. On a studio day for *Birds* we'd be picked up at some horribly early hour and driven in so we'd get our breakfast at the canteen when we arrived. We'd worked at Elstree for years when one morning I happened to be behind Lesley in the queue for breakfast. She filled her tray up and just walked off.

I said, ''Ere, you didn't pay for that!'

She looked at me blankly. 'I didn't know I had to,' she replied.

'We've been here for two years and you've never paid for your breakfast?!'

No one had ever dared to ask her for the money. Honestly, she got away with things that no one else would and she flounced about none the wiser. If that had been me or Pauline, they would have chased us up the street.

Kiffy Swash

Kiffy is Joe Swash's mum and is one of my oldest and most loyal friends.

She's a wise old bird and we've known each other since

our kids were little – Lauren is about the same age as Joe so they were mates and she's also close to Casey who is Kiffy's second oldest. Kiffy's youngest, Shana, and my Louis are the same age and they grew up together as well, and it's always been one of those really easy friendships which just works.

I wish I'd kept the tapes we made of the kids when they were younger. Lauren and her cousins wanted to be the Spice Girls and they said Joe could be in the group, but he would have to audition first. He really wanted to be in the band but he can't sing – he's tone deaf – and so the girls never let him pass the audition.

He also lost his virginity in my house in Devonia Road. We were always having parties and there was one time we realized Joe and my neighbour's daughter had gone missing.

The kids were going, 'Mum, Mum, Joe's in the toilet with so-and-so', and so we started knocking on the door, asking what the hell was going on and to get out because people needed to use the loo.

He came out with a big red face, bless him. And none of us will ever let him forget it. He's a good boy is Joe.

Kiffy's been an amazing mum to her kids and she's done it alone. Her husband Ricky, who was a taxi driver and a really fit and healthy bloke, went to bed one night and started making these strange noises. It turned out to be his heart.

My sister Debbie lives next door and went round when she heard the shouting and screaming. The paramedics worked on him but it was too late. He was only thirty-nine. Joe was just eleven and from then on he kind of took over as the head of the family and looked after them all.

Kiffy is a straight-down-the-line kind of woman and knows what to say in a crisis. We've been on loads of holidays together, renting apartments in the same complex and there are three generations of us now so we go away with our kids and grandkids in tow as well. I wouldn't be without her.

Lynne Gammon

Lynne is my hairdresser and has been for decades. She's from Hoxton so even more Cockney than me if you can believe that.

We met in the late eighties because Mark was friends with her husband Geoff and we used to have nights out the four of us. Me and Lynne hit it off from the start and when we get together we never shut up.

Her mum was called Joyce, a fantastic woman who we used to call the Queen of F***ing Everything. She had perfectly styled bleached blonde hair and all the surfaces in her house were covered in china figurines with festoon curtains at every window – she was the Barbara Cartland of Hoxton. Joyce used to have all the shoplifters come to her with the stuff they'd nicked and she'd sell it on for them.

Lynne definitely inherited Joyce's knack for wheeling and dealing. My old friend at *Loose Women* Carol McGiffin kept saying she wanted 'Linda Robson hair' because she really liked my colour. I asked her how much she paid for hers and she said £400 because obviously she was going to some fancy London salon who see their customers coming a mile off.

I said, 'My mate Lynne Gammon comes round my house and does it.'

She asked me for Lynne's number and booked an appointment, not that Lynne needed the extra business because she has loads of regulars keeping her busy. Most of them are members of my family. Anyway, she did a great job on Carol's hair and Carol was really pleased with it – she kept on sending me pictures of her new do. 'And it only cost me fifty quid!' she said.

'That's hilarious,' I replied. 'Because she only charges me thirty!'

Carol was outraged. Nicely played, Lynne!

We once took a motorhome to the south of France for a week when our kids were younger. The van broke down so I had to go and find someone with spark plugs in France in the middle of nowhere. Lynne stayed with the kids and off I went, trying to mime 'spark plugs' to bemused French people.

Somehow I found someone who came and got the van started, but then we didn't dare switch the engine off in case it conked out again. We pulled into a shopping centre and left it running while we went in because we were so worried! There were so many dramas on that holiday but we had such a good time.

Lynne lives over in Hackney now so we don't see as much of each other as we used to, but she's one of my rocks because we've been through a lot together. Her sister got breast cancer and I was with Lynne the night she died.

And when I wasn't well a few years ago she came down to the Priory to do my hair.

'F***ing hell, look at the state of her!' she'd say.

She's a rough diamond with a heart of gold and I love her to bits.

Jackie Dardis

My cousin Jackie Dardis is more like a sister to me, Tina and Debbie. Her dad Sean was my mum's brother and he was the first one of Nanny Dardis's thirteen kids to die. I mentioned earlier that he passed away the week I was getting married to Mark.

She's got four sisters and a brother, and when they were kids the family moved out to Chingford, which felt like the countryside to us. It's why we nicknamed her the Big Essex Tart.

Jackie was always a bit of a rebel. She met this boy called Larry when she was still a teenager and left home and lived in a car with him for about six months.

She's had a lot of heartache in her life but she's a fighter. One night she'd just sat down to start watching *I'm a Celebrity . . . Get Me Out of Here!* when she collapsed on the floor. She woke up just as it was finishing, so she'd been passed out like that for an hour. She called for an ambulance but was told there was a bit of a wait so she got in her car and drove herself to hospital, where she was later diagnosed with a brain tumour. She very nearly died.

I went to visit her in the hospital and you could see where they'd cut the tumour out because her head was all shaved. Poor Jackie couldn't even speak properly at first and we thought she'd never be the same again. But she recovered and bounced back. And then she got breast cancer. How much is one person expected to take?

She went through treatment for that and had one of her breasts removed and, touch wood, she's fit and well now.

We do everything together. She was with me and my sisters when Mum and Dad died and is included in everything we do. Always will be.

Tina and Debbie

Me and my sisters have completely different personalities, but we couldn't be closer if we tried. We would do anything for each other and the bonds between us are even stronger since we lost Mum.

We've supported each other through a lot of sadness, particularly when in 2015 Tina found a lump in her breast and was sent to get it checked out. The doctor said it was a cyst and nothing to worry about, so she phoned to tell me the good news and said she was going to open the champagne.

About half an hour later, she called back and said the champagne wasn't going to be opened after all because they'd found something else behind the cyst. It was stage 2 breast cancer and so she had to go through a lumpectomy and then several months of chemotherapy and radiotherapy.

I felt desperate for her. It came only a year after her

husband Sergio had died – remember they'd been together since they were teenagers when everyone said they'd never last? They'd been together more than forty years when they were having dinner one evening and Serge stood up to say he was going to get a shower but just dropped to the kitchen floor right in front of Tina. That was it. He was fifty-five.

She'd rung me and said, 'I think Sergio's dead.'

Tina can sometimes be a little dramatic, so I thought she was putting it on a bit, but me and Debbie got in the car and drove over there and by the time we arrived it was confirmed that he'd gone. The paramedics had tried to revive him but it was no good.

Tina will never get over it. They had made such a lovely life together. Serge had done a self-build out in Essex and he'd managed all that on top of his day job, so he was a really hard worker. She still has the handkerchief he used, still got his dressing gown. She lives on her own now and so we go and stay with her quite a lot to keep her company. Tina says she will never meet anyone who measures up to Serge, so she'll be on her own for the rest of her life.

After all her treatment she's now cancer-free and I'm so proud of her.

Her daughter Annika has since had breast cancer too. She was just thirty-nine when she was diagnosed in 2020. Poor Annika went through treatment and chemo during Covid, which was a tough and lonely journey for her. She's doing amazingly well now, thank God. She doesn't drink and she runs every day, so she's fit and strong and has made a full recovery. She's a strong woman, just like her mum.

Most of my colleagues at *Loose Women* have become great mates off screen, which makes going into work an absolute joy. Nadia Sawalha is one of the most beautiful women I know, all lovely and voluptuous with gorgeous curly hair. She's just very family-orientated and we get on really well.

Kaye Adams is a little darling and an amazing anchor because she always stays really calm. She's got the figure of an eighteen-year-old but she's actually really insecure about her body, which I think is mad. Did you see her on *Strictly Come Dancing*? Legs for days! I was so gutted for her to be the first one out because I think she could have had a great experience on there if she'd had half a chance.

I rang her straight after watching her lose the dance-off to Matt Goss and I said, 'Kaye, you were f***ing robbed.'

Denise Welch is a completely different woman compared to when I first started working with her. Denise and Carol McGiffin were a bit like a pair of ladettes back then, out every night drinking, but now she's squeaky clean.

Someone else I adore is Janet Street-Porter, who has a sharp tongue but a soft heart. She's so intelligent and can make me change my mind on an issue I'd thought I was dead set on. We need someone like Janet on the team because she will be the most vocal when we need to make a case to the producers.

She mentioned once on television that she hated Halloween and trick or treaters. She doesn't live far from me so that Halloween night I went round her house with the *Scream* mask on and knocked on the door. She told me to 'f*** off'.

I have to keep her in check sometimes because I don't think she means to be rude to people, but it can come across like that. She just says exactly what she thinks and she has her little ways, but occasionally I'll tell her, 'Oi! Say sorry!'

I think she's mellowed a lot in the last couple of years and she does have such a lovely life. She'll come into work wearing the most gorgeous coat and I'll say, 'Ooh, that's beautiful. Where'd you get it from?'

And she'll say, 'Ellie gave it to me.' As in Elton John. She has very famous mates.

I had a dream once that I had sex with Elton on the Eurostar. Every detail was so real that when I woke up it took me a few seconds to register that it hadn't actually happened.

Simone, who does our hair and make-up at *Loose Women*, also works with Elton a lot and she flies with him in his private jet. So I gave her a note to pass to him which read, *Dear Elton, I loved your book* Rocket Man. *Do you remember when we had sex on the Eurostar (in my dreams)? Love Linda*

He sent me one back saying, *Dear Linda, It wasn't the Eurostar. It was the Orient Express and we made so much noise that they chucked us off!*

I've still got the letter; I'll always keep that. I'm a huge fan of Elton and my aim in life is to meet him in person.

Janet has promised me that before I die she'll introduce us, but it hasn't happened yet.

Charlene White is another great anchor and there's something a bit naughty about her as well. I think she quite likes to party.

Christine Lampard is probably the nicest woman on television and she comes along to show her support at everything everyone has going on outside of *Loose Women*, whether that's a book or clothing range launch. She comes in on her days off to celebrate birthdays and she gives such generous gifts.

I was on holiday in Majorca a couple of years ago and me, Mark and the kids were sitting in a restaurant when this car screeched to a halt and out jumped Christine and Frank Lampard. She'd spotted me and they came and joined us. All the waiters were wanting selfies with Frank and we had a lovely time with them.

And then there's Stacey Solomon, who is the loveliest girl. She was quite nervous when she started but she's really come into her own as a Loose Woman and I was so happy when she got together with Joe Swash, who, as you know, I've known his whole life through my friendship with Kiffy. Stacey might come across as ditzy but people underestimate her – she's got her head screwed on, that girl. I was the only Loose Woman to go to Stacey and Joe's wedding at Pickle Cottage in July 2022. It was the most beautiful day and those two are just perfect for each other.

Jane Moore has been a big support to me recently as I've been working through some family issues; she's been such a good friend. And Ruth Langsford is someone else

I always like being on the show with. I was really sad when Ruth and her husband Eamonn Holmes were moved aside on *This Morning* on Fridays to make way for Dermot O'Leary and Alison Hammond. I love Alison and Dermot and they do work well as a partnership, but Ruth and Eamonn had been there for years, filling in at every holiday and the crew adored them.

My mum always had a soft spot for Eamonn. Once I was flying out to Belfast to present a community award and I took my mum along with me. Carol Smillie was on the flight as well as Kerry Katona and Eamonn, and we were all going to the same event.

Eamonn saw me and Mum and offered us a lift in his cab, explaining he'd have to go via his house so he could pick up a pair of shoes. My mum was beside herself with excitement. When he popped into the house for the shoes, she rang Beryl from the bingo and said, 'You'll never guess where I am right now . . . ?'

We went to the bar after the awards and Eamonn's family were all there and he made a bit of a fuss of my mum because I'd told him how much she liked him. My mum had the best night of her life and I'll never forget that.

Kelly Holmes

By the time I got to my early sixties, I didn't think I had room in my life for any more new friends. But I hadn't banked on meeting Kelly Holmes.

You know when you just instantly click with someone?

It's also been lovely to discover that you're never too old to welcome new people into your life and the heart is never too full – it just expands to fit everyone in.

Me and Kelly first met properly at Pride in 2022. ITV had a big rainbow bus and I gave Kelly's girlfriend my pass to get her on. We were having a really good day but then the bus broke down and we ended up having to walk. We saw each other again a few days later at the British LGBT Awards when we were sitting at the same table and we had the best night and swapped numbers.

She called me a few days later to say ITV had approached her to join the *Loose Women* panel and could I meet her to talk it through before she went in to see the bosses. So I went down to this posh private club in Covent Garden where she's a member and we just got on really, really well.

I told her all about life at *Loose* and how you get to the studio in time for the morning meeting, then into make-up, then into another meeting (there are LOADS of meetings), do the show and then you go home! We talked for ages and she told me all about her girlfriend (those two are so good together) and we've just been great friends ever since. I love it when we're on the show together and we always end up going out to eat afterwards on those days.

She's so thoughtful and kind – I collect teapots and she bought me three, one red, one white and one blue, and a cup with the number '1809', which was the number she ran with when she won double gold at the 2004 Olympics.

I'm so grateful that we met and I know she's going to be a mate for ever.

Brenda Edwards

I love Brenda so much – I've been to see her in every theatre production she's ever done. She has the most enormous talent. I don't think she knows just how good she is.

For a lot of us Loose Women, the show has been an anchor for us through extremely difficult times personally and I know it's been really important to Brenda since her lovely son Jamal died suddenly in February 2022 aged just thirty-one.

She came back to the show after two months because she needed the routine and focus being at work gave her, as well as the comfort and strength she drew from being around all of us who love and support her. Jamal was such a special young man and he and Louis had a really lovely friendship, formed over their mutual love of music.

The day after he died I went straight over to Brenda's after doing *Loose Women* with some flowers. I said I wouldn't stay, but I just wanted her to know she was in my thoughts.

She was sitting on the stairs and insisted I come in. 'Don't you dare cry,' she said.

I promised I wouldn't.

Brenda's house had always been such a happy, bright and colourful home, but that day it felt very different. The shutters were down at the windows so it was dark, and it was so cold. I didn't stay very long, but we had a chat and she knew I'd be there for her if she needed anything.

With Mother's Day approaching, which I knew would be extremely hard for Brenda, I went to John Lewis on Oxford Street to get a parcel of lovely things for her. One of the assistants asked if she could help and I said my friend had just lost her son and I wanted to get her a care package for Mother's Day.

This lady helped me put together a big hamper of goodies like face cream, chocolates and candles, and then she refused to let me pay for it.

I took it round to Brenda's the next day. I knocked on the door and Brenda's daughter Tanisha answered.

I said, 'I wanted to leave these here for Mummy. Can you tell her I didn't pay for it? John Lewis gifted it.'

The way Brenda has coped and how she is making sure that Jamal lives on through the Jamal Edwards Self Belief Trust is completely heroic. It's the same sort of strength and determination that I've seen in the Kinsellas. Though they are wracked with grief for their lost children, their resilience never fails to amaze me.

There's Always One
(and It's Usually Me)

Havoc at Richard Branson's house

I'm always getting into trouble. I can't help it. I'm just one of those people who attracts it and I end up in a pickle whatever I'm doing.

In the mid-nineties me and Pauline were filming *Jobs for the Girls* and we had to go to Richard Branson's house for an episode on party planning. It was in Notting Hill or somewhere nice like that and he'd knocked two houses together to make one massive place. It was really beautiful, as you can imagine, full of expensive furniture, art on the walls and loads of fancy china.

I was admiring it all and, as I turned to walk up the stairs, I somehow (and don't ask me how because to this day I haven't got a clue how I managed it) knocked over a vase and it smashed into smithereens all over the floor.

Time seemed to go into slow motion. I looked at Pauline, who was standing there with her mouth wide open in shock. I turned to my left and right, half expecting Jeremy Beadle to appear. And then I did the only thing I ever do when I'm nervous and caught in a difficult or compromising situation – I burst out laughing.

Richard came through and said, 'Oh, don't worry, don't worry! It's fine!'

'I'm so sorry, Richard,' I said. 'I don't know how that happened.'

I offered to buy him a new one but thank God he didn't take me up on that because it wasn't going to have been something he'd picked up at a car boot sale.

A lady member of staff came scuttling through with a dustpan and brush to clear up the mess and it was gone in a matter of seconds. Richard was such a gent about it but I felt so bad.

A few years later, I was in Marbella with the family and he was in the same restaurant as us.

My mum said, 'There's your mate over there, Lin. Go and say hello!'

'He's not really my mate, Mum.'

'Course he is. Go on! Go and say hello and tell him I'm your mother.' And she was virtually pushing me out of my chair.

He was with his wife and kids and I didn't want to disturb them. I also didn't fancy being introduced as the woman who had destroyed some irreplaceable family heirloom so I kept my head down and left him to it!

Scooter off

If there's an accident to have or an undignified exit to make, then you can bet your bottom dollar I'll claim it. The whole family was out in Murcia in Spain for my brother-in-law Tommy's sixtieth birthday and we were gathered in this big square when my nephew, Little Tom, turned up on this electric scooter.

'Do you want a go?' he asked.

'Go on, then,' I said, climbing on board.

I didn't realize it was electric so there's me, trying to push down on the pedals and turning the handlebars and this thing just took off. I ran my nephew Teddy's girl-friend over as the scooter shot across the square and I ended up in the middle of this very public place on my knees with my arse in the air and my dress over my head giving everyone a flash of my big black knickers.

I'd actually really hurt myself but I couldn't get up, partly because of the pain but mostly because I was laughing so much. Two of my nephews came running over to pick me up – everyone else was doubled over in knots and couldn't move for laughing.

All the people in the surrounding restaurants had stopped eating and were gawping at this complete spec-tacle. At least I provided them with some entertainment during their meals.

What a mug!

I've got a very sensitive nose and I can sniff out offensive smells from a mile off. One night I was upstairs in bed with all three kids and I could smell s*** coming from downstairs. Our dog George was only a puppy so I knew he was the culprit.

I put on my dressing gown, went downstairs and cleared it all up and put it into the nearest bag I could find, which happened to be one from Selfridges because I'd been out shopping that day.

I opened the front door, looked around to check no one was watching and then went to run across the road to put it in a skip which was outside the church opposite. I know you're not supposed to do that, but I didn't really want the poo in my bin! I'm my mother's daughter – what can I say?

Just as I stepped out into the street, someone wearing a hoodie and riding a mountain bike sped up to me, punched me in the face and stole the Selfridges bag out of my hand. It all happened so fast that I didn't have time to see if it was a man, woman, boy or girl, but whoever it was, they left me with a big black eye and I was really shaken up.

We called the police but they didn't have enough to go on to have any hope of catching who did it. I was due to film something the next day but had to cancel that because my face was such a mess.

The one silver lining (and something that still makes me smile now) was the thought of this thug feeling all pleased with themselves for grabbing this Selfridges bag, imagining what expensive treats might be inside and then reaching in to get a handful of s***.

If you're reading this now, it serves you right!

Accidental front-page splash

I ended up on the front page of a newspaper once because me and Debbie had gone to see Robbie Williams in concert at Wembley and caused a bit of controversy.

What happened was Robbie kicked a football into the

crowd and this woman and me both went for it at the same time. I caught it and I gave it to my sister because she was an even bigger Robbie fan than me. This woman then went to the papers and said I had knocked her to the floor just to get this football! As if.

The article was accompanied by a photo of her looking all frail and dishevelled and with a walking stick, which I definitely hadn't seen at Wembley, making it look like I'd knocked over a disabled woman. Anyone who knows me knows that's simply not in my nature. I would never do anything like that.

Anyway, we gave a no comment to the story (I think my exact words were 'Go f*** yourself', which is the same comment I give to every newspaper story that's a load of rubbish) and we've still got the football. Which I won fair and square, by the way.

In full swing

I chat to anyone and collect friends wherever I go, often much to Mark's annoyance. We once met this couple on holiday and got really friendly with them, so I gave them my number before we came home.

A few weeks later they gave me a ring and invited us both to a little party at their place down in Kent and I said that would be lovely, but Mark really didn't want to go. I eventually persuaded him to come along and when we arrived, there were about three other couples and the atmosphere was slightly uneasy, like there was a bit of tension in the air.

The next thing I knew, they were putting their car keys on the table. Me being me, I didn't immediately twig what was happening, but I was aware that Mark was looking over at me, desperately trying to catch my eye to signal that we had to make our excuses and leave.

He suddenly stood up and said we had to go because his brother's Rottweiler had escaped and was on the loose.

'But, Mark,' I said, all confused and still not grasping what was going on, 'your brother ain't got a Rottweiler!'

If looks could kill! Mark was hurriedly putting his coat on and I knew I had to follow him out because he was driving home. Thinking about it, that was just as well because if I'd had the car keys on me, I'd probably have copied the others and chucked them in and then God knows what would have happened!

We got out of there and Mark was hopping mad with me all the way home.

'You brought us to a swingers' party! What have I told you? Don't keep giving people your phone number!'

They were perfectly nice people and they must have got the wrong end of the stick about us. And us them for that matter! Because we definitely weren't into what they were clearly into, I can promise you that.

You're fired!

When we were on the Aussie tour of *Grumpy Old Women*, I ended up nearly burning the apartment down at the complex we were staying in. We'd not long arrived in Oz and the kids were both jet-lagged and sleeping it off.

I thought I'd pop some of those potato smiley faces in the oven for them and then have a walk down to get a coffee for myself.

Typical me, I ended up chatting to some air steward and completely forgetting all about the kids' dinner. When I got back, the fire brigade was there and the whole building had been evacuated.

I knew it was me.

Jenny did too. 'You've nearly killed your kids!' she said, jumping up and down.

Everyone was safe, thank God, but I felt terrible.

Flight risk

Mark has never really liked flying but he especially hates flying with me because there's always a drama. I'd always get him to the airport six hours before the flight because I'd mucked up the times.

One of my worst airport cock-ups was when we were headed up to Newcastle for the second run of the *Birds of a Feather* theatre show in May 2013 and I was supposed to be meeting Pauline and her husband Steve, who was one of our producers, at London City Airport to travel together.

I was running late and arrived just as the barrier to the gate came down. The staff were really lovely, but they said it was automatic and all done on computers so they couldn't override it. I had no option but to wait for the next flight, which was at 2 p.m. and would still get me to the Theatre Royal in Newcastle for the show at 7 p.m.

I rang our company manager Antony who thought I was playing tricks on him when I said I'd missed the flight, and then went to sit in the Jamie Oliver restaurant and had a scroll through my phone. I was quite enjoying myself.

I headed to the gate about half an hour before the flight, sat myself down and tweeted something like: *Looking forward to seeing everyone in Newcastle tonight. Hope everyone enjoys the show. Can't wait!*

I noticed that we hadn't been called up to board the plane, so I asked the bloke sitting next to me if the flight to Newcastle had been delayed.

He said, 'Er, this one is going to Rio.'

I was sitting at the wrong gate and the Newcastle plane had left three minutes ago, which meant I had managed to miss two flights in one day. I couldn't believe it.

I went back to the BA desk and they were sympathetic but also laughing because they'd never had anyone miss two flights when they were actually in the terminal at the time.

There were no other flights to Newcastle until the following day, so the best alternative was to fly to Glasgow and then get a cab to Newcastle, which cost me £400. I arrived at the theatre just in time to watch the audience coming out after the show. Oh God, I felt awful.

I went up to the bar and Lesley was crying because she'd never been so scared in her life when they'd realized I wasn't going to make it.

My understudy, who was an actress called Penelope Woodman, had stepped in and she was quite posh, so they hadn't really known what to expect when she became Tracey. Anyway, apparently she was very good. Pauline and Lesley said, 'She's f***ing better than you!'

I didn't dare tell the family what had happened in case they had me locked up.

Mistaken identity

I was in Selfridges one day with Louis and I spotted Peter Jackson, director, screenwriter and producer of the *Lord of the Rings* film trilogy. I'm never one to waste an opportunity to say hello so I went up to him and said, 'Excuse me, Peter. This is my son and he's a big fan of *Lord of the Rings* . . .'

I turned to Louis, who was pink-cheeked with embarrassment and said, 'Speak Elvish to him, Lou. Go on!'

Then I turned back to Peter and said, 'Honestly, he's your biggest fan, Peter. We went to the premiere and everything. Louis, speak Elvish!'

And Peter looked me in the eye and said, 'Linda, I'm not who you think I am. I'm Stephen Poliakoff and I live on your street.'

Well, that stopped me in my tracks. I started laughing and so did Stephen so he took it well. Louis said he was never coming out with me again.

I swear, though, if you look at pictures of Peter Jackson and Stephen Poliakoff, they are like twins. So in my defence it was an easy mistake to make . . .

And another one

I was guilty of another, much more unforgivable case of mistaken identity when I was at Arsenal's Emirates

Stadium for the topping-out ceremony in 2005. I was filming a little segment for *The One Show* when a tall, slim bloke who I recognized was coming towards me and I said, 'Hello, Sven, how are you?' I thought it was Sven-Göran Eriksson.

The kids were there and they looked horrified. 'Mum! That's Arsène Wenger!'

You'd think coming from a family of Arsenal fans I'd have known that. Anyway, he was laughing, but the kids wanted to kill me.

I had to interview Thierry Henry as part of the same film (tough job, that one!) who is the most beautiful man inside and out. He's so handsome.

'*Bonjour*, Thierry,' I greeted him.

'*Bonjour*, Linda!' he said. And then he started speaking French to me.

I asked him if he spoke Cockney.

'Not since Ray Parlour left,' he replied.

I bumped into him about a year later at the Landmark Hotel in central London – he gave me a wave and another '*Bonjour*, Linda!' and came over for a chat. Such a nice man. And that French accent, honestly . . . It sends me weak at the knees.

Anyway, we were all at this topping-out ceremony and they were burying a time capsule which was filled with meaningful items from people attached to the club. Thierry put a pair of his trademark over-the-knee socks in there, Gunners fan author Nick Hornby put one of his books in and Arsenal legend Charlie George put in a football shirt.

I managed to get a picture of me, the three kids and

Mark in that time capsule, which is now buried under the stadium. And I always imagine in 150 years it'll get dug up and they'll go, 'Who the f***'s that?!'

Social media drama

Me and social media are not a good mix. These days Bobbie Girl takes care of all of that for me, which is a weight off because I'm hopeless with that kind of thing. Also, there's an addictive streak in me, which meant for a while my Twitter usage got a bit out of control and I had to take a step back from it.

When I first started on Twitter and Instagram and had about fifty followers, I really enjoyed it. I got to know everyone on there and loved chatting to them. But as both accounts started to grow, it was getting harder to reply to all my mentions and it was causing issues in my marriage.

Me and Mark would be sitting watching a film and I'd be tweeting someone and he'd get really cross with me. 'What's the point of watching something together if you're going to be sat on your phone all night?' he'd say.

And he was right. But it was like an addiction and it had taken over my life. I used to get sucked into sob stories and would end up sending complete strangers money because I hate to think of people suffering when I could help. I paid £3,000 for someone's cancer treatment once. Another time a single mum approached me pleading poverty and I sent her cash and a load of baby clothes.

One person who had really bad anxiety and depression contacted me and I paid for him to have treatment at the Linden Centre in London. The kids would go mad with me.

'Mum!' they'd say. 'There's something not right with you!'

But I just want to help people, and social media was making it easy for them to get in touch with me.

The thing that ended my love affair with it was a dilemma we were discussing on *Loose Women* on the back of a news story where a woman had been prosecuted for failing to hand in a twenty-pound note she'd found on a shop floor.

We were asked, if we'd walked into a shop and seen the twenty pounds on the floor, what would we do?

I said I would always hand it in, especially if it was a shop like the one in the story, which looked quite 'poor'. I said it obviously wasn't Waitrose or Marks & Spencer, so it was likely that the person who had dropped it didn't have very much money.

Oh my God, the backlash was like nothing I'd ever experienced before. I was getting called all the names under the sun by people in Stoke-on-Trent who thought I'd insulted their town.

I hadn't even known the shop was in Stoke! It could have been anywhere for all I knew; I was just making the point that the shop obviously wasn't a posh one. I've done panto in Stoke-on-Trent and loved it there.

I was getting so much abuse and I was really, really upset about it. I'd only ever been positive on my social media and I'd never had any trouble on there before.

While all this was raging on, I was assured by ITV that I'd said and done nothing wrong and that no one was cross with me. The trolling and the horrible tweets just wouldn't stop, though, and so in the end I decided to come off Twitter and I've never tweeted since.

My Ben Shephard crush

I've always had a soft spot for Ben Shephard. I know he's happily married and quite a few years younger than me, but he's lovely and (after Donny Osmond) is my not-so-secret celebrity crush. He was the main reason I accepted a job doing *Tipping Point: Lucky Stars* in 2016.

At the studios there was a big blown-up photo of him in the corridor looking very gorgeous, so I got my lipstick out and drew a big speech bubble coming out of his mouth saying: *I love Linda Robson.*

Right at that moment, he walked round the corner and caught me in the act.

I gulped.

'That, Linda,' he said, 'is absolutely correct!'

So, watch this space, one day we might just run away into the sunset together.

Caught short

You know those toilets you get on trains with the electronic sliding door which you have to press a button to lock? Someone as accident-prone and technophobic as me is always going to come a cropper with that sort of modern-day invention.

There was one time me and Andrea McLean went up to Manchester to do some filming for *Loose Women*. I miss Andrea since she left the show in 2020. She's doing really well for herself and is so happy with her husband Nick. And she's gorgeous, of course – Andrea has always been even more beautiful in real life.

Anyway, on the train home, I went to the loo and I'm sitting there mid-flow when a recorded message comes on to say the door is not locked.

'S***!' I screamed.

So I stand up in a panic, trousers and knickers round my ankles and weeing all over the floor (because when you've had three kids, once you start, you can't stop) as I desperately try to reach the lock button. Unfortunately it's not the lock button I manage to press but the one that opens the door.

Oh. My. God.

The door slides open, almost in slow motion, and standing there is the ticket inspector and the rest of the carriage, including Andrea, staring back at me.

'I suppose you want to see my ticket?' is the only thing I can think of to say.

Me and Andrea still laugh about that now. She was helpless with laughter at the time, as was the inspector and all the other passengers. It's a good job I can take a joke, isn't it?

The Birds are Back in Town

A faltering start

There had been rumours for years about a possible stage production of *Birds of a Feather* but they never came to anything. I was excited by the prospect but after a while I stopped getting my hopes up and assumed it was one of those things that would never happen.

However, in 2009, I dared to believe again when we heard that the Comedy Theatre Company, who had already put on successful stage versions of *Dinnerladies* and *Keeping up Appearances*, had snapped it up and were going to produce it. Yes, at last! After a thirteen-year absence, *Birds of a Feather* was back.

The excitement and anticipation I felt – that we all felt – about breathing life back into *Birds of a Feather* again were off the scale and we couldn't wait to give the fans what they'd spent years patiently waiting for. We were also eager to introduce Sharon, Tracey and Dorien to a whole new generation and we wondered if it might, just might, lead to a long overdue return to TV.

But it didn't take long for us to come crashing back down to earth. The whole production started off on a bad foot because the original *Birds of a Feather* creators and writers had a vision for the revival that didn't seem to involve me, Pauline and Lesley. Apparently they thought the show needed new talent in order to attract a fresh audience and after a series of conversations it became clear they had plans to recast the main roles. They seemed to be giving different reasons depending on who they were talking to and they were playing us all off against each other. Did they honestly think the three of us wouldn't get together and compare notes?

Lesley phoned me and Pauline and told us that they'd said to her that me and Pauline were out.

'Well, they told us they were going to recast Dorien,' I said.

We were all good friends, so obviously we were going to share that information with each other. In the end we confronted the producers and said either all of us did it or none of us and they backed down. We knew our worth and that the people coming to see the show would want all three of us up on that stage.

The next issue was the script. The theatre production originally wasn't going to be written by Laurence and Maurice – at that point their role was just going to be overseeing everything. So this other bloke wrote the scripts, sent them over and they were completely s***. The storyline centred on this fella Tracey was seeing who had a twin brother, and I'm sorry but it just wasn't funny.

As soon as the three of us read it we said absolutely no way. To go out with a substandard script like that would have been letting down all the people who had watched and enjoyed the show and supported us over the years. It wasn't up to scratch at all.

It didn't help that the producers working on it didn't

seem to be interested in my views. They had arranged a meeting with Lesley in Soho House to discuss the problems with the script and said me and Pauline didn't need to come.

Pauline was filming *Emmerdale* so couldn't make it anyway, but Lesley told me I should be there and to come along despite what the producers had said. So I kind of gatecrashed this meeting where they proceeded to disregard almost every suggestion I made, like I should have no say in what was happening. I think they thought I was stupid and would have nothing constructive to add. But I'm not stupid and I had a lot to say. I've been in this business a long time and I know what I'm doing.

We weren't making unreasonable demands. We just wanted the show to be good and we knew the script was wrong. Me and Lesley told the producers that we weren't doing it unless they got Laurence and Maurice to write it, even though they seemed as if they didn't want to involve us a few months earlier. And after some toing and froing they agreed.

Laurence and Maurice weren't getting let off the hook, though.

I said to Laurence when I saw him, 'You should be ashamed of yourself. We've always been f***ing loyal to you and Maurice.'

To be fair, he owned it and he was apologetic. But we'd been really upset.

There was another spanner in the works with Pauline being up in Leeds filming *Emmerdale* where she had joined the permanent cast, which meant that she wasn't available. It seemed to be delay after delay in getting it off the ground and I did start to wonder if it was doomed after all.

Weighty matters

In 2011 Pauline announced she was leaving *Emmerdale* and finally it looked like we might be able to start moving.

Now, like a lot of women, I've spent most of my life on one sort of diet or another, even when I probably didn't need to. I've done WeightWatchers and used slimming pills – I've tried just about every one available and they're all horrible. They either give you diarrhoea or they send you hyper.

My weight has yo-yoed so much over the years. After I had Lauren, I went straight back to a size ten within a month. But when I had Louis, possibly because I'd also packed up smoking and was eating more to compensate, I put on four stone and it took me ages to lose weight after that. In the mid-nineties I did a weight-loss video called *Light as a Feather* which combined Pilates and a low-calorie diet, and I wasn't even really that big then. As part of the contract, wherever I was in the country filming, they'd send a bike with my diet food, which had been tailored to me and what I liked.

Pauline used to say, 'Look at you getting your bloody food delivered every day!'

She was always the one who was most targeted by the press about her weight, but I remember the TV critic Garry Bushell writing a horrible piece after the first couple of series saying Chigwell wasn't doing us any favours because we'd all piled on the pounds. And there was once a double-page spread in the paper saying I'd got fat, using a pap shot which I'm sure they'd deliberately made look wider. I was on a plane going up to Scotland the day it came out and I remember seeing the other passengers reading that article and just wanting to curl up, feeling awful about myself.

By 2011 I was over fourteen stone and it was the first time in all the years we'd been friends that Pauline was smaller than me. She'd been based up north filming *Emmerdale* so we'd not really seen each other for the best part of twelve months and while I knew she'd been on this diet and was losing a bit of weight, nothing could have prepared me for seeing her transformation in the flesh. I was shocked. She'd lost eight and a half stone in the space of a year. She looked like a completely different person.

I knew we were going to be doing the tour in a few months' time and I didn't want the focus to be on how much weight I'd put on. So I got on the same diet plan as Pauline, and managed to lose three stone in as many months.

The plan was so strict and the side effects I experienced were revolting. My hair started falling out, my breath stank and because I was literally living on packet soups, a snack bar and a milkshake (that's all I would have all day). I was starving the whole time.

It's not sustainable and I knew I couldn't last on it forever. As soon as I started eating like a normal person again, the weight went back on. It was never going to be a long-term solution, but I needed a quick fix and it served that purpose.

I'm fine with where my figure is now. I'm always going to have a bit of a tummy. I get that from my mum. But I'm vegetarian and I don't drink alcohol or fizzy drinks. I like the odd biscuit because you can't deny yourself all life's pleasures. I'm never going to wear a bikini again, but I'm very happy in my swimming costume.

Friends reunited

Once Laurence and Maurice got involved with the script, the whole show was revolutionized – when we got it, we knew it was good. It started off with Tracey and Sharon getting a letter saying Dorien was in an old people's home. So we go down to visit but it turns out she's not a resident there, she actually owns the place, and the whole thing was just really, really funny. Just like the old days.

When rehearsals started it was like saying hello again to three old friends – Tracey, Sharon and Dorien – and we slipped straight back into the roles as second nature. My God, we'd missed them!

Pauline's boy Charlie Quirke was cast in the role of Tracey's younger son Travis, and across four months we took the show all over the country, spending about a week in each place. It felt lovely to be back together.

In between the two shows a day, Lesley would be in her dressing room exercising, which is how she stays so trim. While she was doing her aerobics, I used to go shopping and Pauline would have a sleep on the fold-up mattress she took with her everywhere. She probably needed the nap to help her calm down, because Pauline had never been so scared.

Remember I told you how much she hated doing that panto at the Hackney Empire back in 1991? The nerves were exactly the same as they had been then, maybe even worse.

She used to work herself up into a right frenzy each night. Me and Lesley tried to reassure her by reminding her that we'd all be there together if anything went wrong and that we'd chip in and get through it. We knew each other so well that it would be easy to do that, but she couldn't calm her anxiety.

On the first night in March 2012 in Leatherhead everything that could go wrong did go wrong. We had so many hiccups. For a start I dried and completely forgot my lines. I fell back on my theory that if you bring the audience in, you'll be OK, so I just said, 'Right, I ain't got a clue what I say here. Could someone tell me?'

The audience loved it.

But there were issues with the sound and all sorts, and by the time we came to do the curtain call on that opening night I think our nerves were shot. Thankfully it seemed that we'd got all the little snags out of the way from the off and the rest of the tour was absolutely fine.

A lot of the audience weren't your usual theatregoers and so they'd bring their little packed lunches and be chatting to their neighbour during the show. But it was really quite sweet and we loved it.

What goes on tour . . .

While we were touring, rather than staying in hotels, we'd often stay together in apartments. Pauline would do the cooking, I'd do the cleaning and Lesley would do f*** all. But it was the happiest of times, being back to the three of us, and we reverted to exactly how it had always been.

We still cracked each other up like no one else. Pauline smoked occasionally but she didn't want her son Charlie, who was playing Travis, to know. We were at this theatre somewhere one night and she asked me if I thought that smoking in the dressing-room shower would still set the alarm off seeing as there would be loads of steam and it would all get mixed in.

I'm no scientist but I said I thought she'd probably be OK.

I was wrong. Within a minute the alarms were going crazy. The theatre staff were all scratching their heads and saying they'd never had the fire alarms going off before and asking if someone had been making toast backstage.

Pauline was there going crimson and desperately trying to avoid eye contact with everyone. I said I didn't know what had happened; it was a complete mystery. So I saved her skin that day!

Ending on a sickener

The stage show had been so successful that they brought it back for another run in 2013.

We hadn't gone to Scotland during the first tour because we didn't know if they would be that keen on it up there. But loads of people were getting in touch saying to take it north of the border and so we did, performing in Aberdeen, Edinburgh and Glasgow, and they loved it.

The final leg of the tour was in Eastbourne but it all ended in a bit of a disaster because I got norovirus. Me and Lesley had gone and got fish and chips, as you do when you go to the seaside, but when we got back to the theatre I suddenly felt really bad. I went to the dressing room and just lay down and everyone was asking me if I was OK to do the show. The theatre was packed that night and it was the last date of the tour, so I really didn't want to let people down. I insisted I'd be all right and would plough through it.

I did the first couple of scenes thinking I was going to throw up the entire time until I got to the point where I could feel it coming. I ran off the stage and there was a metal bucket in the wings which I vomited into while my microphone was still switched on. The audience heard the whole thing, but I was too ill to care.

They pulled the curtain down and told me they'd put the understudy on, but I felt a bit better and said I would see if I could continue. Obviously the audience knew I'd been sick so they really appreciated it when I came back on and they gave me a big cheer. The things you do for a round of applause . . .

And the next line that Pauline had was, 'What's for dinner, Trace?' which we couldn't have planned better if we tried, and the audience all started killing themselves laughing.

God knows how, but I did the rest of the show and then got a lift home with Lesley. She'd pulled her wig off so she just had a stocking on her head, just so you can picture the scene.

'Get in the back,' she snapped. 'There's no way you're sitting in the front with me. It's contagious.'

So there's me in Lesley's car throwing up into a bag all the way home. What a picture.

After she dropped me off, I lay on the sofa for about three days. Apart from the pancreatitis, I've not known illness on that scale before. It was horrendous.

Norovirus aside, both tours were roaring successes, and it was on the back of them that the whispers began about the show returning to TV. The ticket sales had proven that there was still a lot of love for Sharon, Trace and Dor, and everyone we'd met up and down the country across the two tours had been asking the same question: when are you coming back to telly?

To be honest, it was a question we were asking too.

Back on the box

It was like everyone was buzzing about *Birds of a Feather* all over again. It hadn't escaped the attention of the TV networks and we found out that the BBC had offered us an hour-long Christmas special.

However, ITV had said they wanted to do eight episodes, and we felt that was the better deal. Over the course of a series the old fans would feel like they were properly getting us back again and the new ones would have a real chance to get to know us. So we made the decision to switch channels and head over to the other side. The three of us had a meeting with the writers and we were all in agreement that we wanted to bring the show right up to date and deal with the issues that would be affecting women of Sharon and Tracey's age.

Years before, we'd covered things like testicular cancer and abortion, which I don't think had ever been done on a sitcom before, so it made sense to tackle subjects that were a bit more hard-hitting. We said we were menopausal women and we wanted the show to reflect that, and so we had HRT patches all over the house and we added little affectations, like I'd be sitting there plucking the hairs out of my chin because that's exactly what I do at home. Little details like that can add so much colour and reality to a show and really do count for a lot.

Pauline's son Charlie got the part of Travis Stubbs and he was really good. I was absolutely delighted to be bringing the show back to television; in my opinion it had been away for too long. We'd really wanted as many of the old team back again as possible – same production staff, camera crew, hair, make-up – and we managed to do that with a lot of them, which was terrific.

I had thought the BBC's offer of just a Christmas special was a bit short-sighted given the amount of interest the stage production had generated, but we were happy to be going to ITV. However, they were being a bit niggly about whether three women of our age would be able to attract a big audience and so they wanted to introduce lots of new, younger supporting characters.

We were happy to give it a go if that's what they thought the show needed, and so they got Tracey's eldest son Garfie back from Australia with his girlfriend and her little girl. I'm not being rude, but the audience only really wanted to see Tracey, Sharon and Dorien sitting around the kitchen island or going to prison visiting the boys.

The young actors they brought in were lovely, but they weren't the reason people watched.

We filmed the series at the ITV Studios and I honestly think those episodes were among the best we ever did. The first episode went out in January 2014 and even though I knew it was good, I was petrified about how it was going to be received. Social media hadn't existed when we'd last been on the telly in 1998, but now people would be tweeting about the show as it happened and there wasn't anything we could do about it.

The kids told me not to log on because there were bound to be a lot of people who didn't like it or professional trolls who just wanted to slag us off for the sake of it, and it wasn't worth getting upset over. As it happened, the response was fantastic. Everyone seemed really happy to have us back and the overall reaction was a huge weight off because we hadn't known what to expect. And ITV commissioned another series, which was amazing.

Me, Pauline and Lesley were given lots of opportunities for input because the writers recognized that we knew these characters better than anyone. So when there was a storyline where Tracey had skin cancer and she got the all-clear, the script said that we should all shout, 'Tracey ain't got cancer!' and then do a conga.

That felt so jarring and wrong.

We said no. That's not right. We wanted it to be bittersweet and have some emotion in there and so it was changed to me saying my results were back and everything was clear and then the three of us joining together in a group hug.

That was the series we won the TV Choice award for Best Comedy in 2016. Finally.

Nearly thirty years after it had all begun, it was about time.

Letting Loose

Getting away with it

Besides *Birds of a Feather*, there is, of course, another huge show which has become so much part of my life I find it hard to separate the two. Becoming a panellist on *Loose Women* has been a roller coaster of a ride and the people I work with there, our loyal viewers and the show itself, have seen me through the best and worst of times over this last decade. I've made friends for life, I've laughed, cried and almost cracked up, and even though it hasn't half got me into hot water on several occasions I wouldn't change it for the world.

I'd first appeared on the show back in 2000 when it was filmed up in Norwich. It was Kaye Adams, Nadia Sawalha and Terri Dwyer who were with me on my debut and I really enjoyed myself. The only thing I didn't like was the 4 a.m. wake-up call to drive you to Norwich. I don't think I could have ever become a regular if the show had stayed there.

When they asked if I would feature on *Loose Women* more frequently in 2012, they'd moved the whole production to the ITV Studios at Waterloo and I was delighted to sign up. For a couple of years before that, because I lived near, I'd been filling in if someone didn't turn up. I remember Lisa Maxwell was snowed in one day and when they rang to ask if I could step in, I was still in my nightdress doing my cleaning. So I was already a semi-regular when I got my contract as a proper member of the team.

I suppose my role there is to speak for the people at home and ask the questions the ordinary man or woman on the street wants answering. I'm not a journalist or an anchor and I'm not very political, although I have always voted. I'm not telling you who for, mind! I might be Mrs Baggy Mouth but I know to keep schtum when it comes to politics. But if I don't understand something, you can be sure there will be plenty of people at home feeling the same way and so my job is to be their voice.

I don't think I've ever been horrible to anyone we've had on, but I feel I can ask things that the others won't.

For some reason people don't seem to be as offended if it comes from me, but I'd never overstep the mark and be mean because we want people to come back on the show. Most of the time anyway!

I'm just a normal nan and mum so it sounds better coming from me than it would Janet Street-Porter who has a journalism background, which makes people a bit more wary. So when we had Andrew Ridgeley on, I asked about what he'd seen of George Michael struggling with his sexuality before he came out. When Nigel Farage was a guest, I asked him, 'What's it like to be the most hated man in Britain?' Dead innocent. That one made the papers the next day and they said that I'd given him 'a grilling'. I wouldn't say that, but I was secretly quite proud of myself that I'd asked the question which had caused a bit of a stir.

To be fair to him, he was very charming about it. I know a lot of people don't like him and they might have good reasons, but I'm not really into politics and I don't read the newspapers so I take people as I find them. I'll always give someone the benefit of the doubt until they prove me otherwise.

Favourite guests

I've heard stories of a chat show presenter on another channel who would go into the guests' dressing rooms before the show and ask if there was anything they didn't want to talk about. He'd then use that against them by bringing up that very thing live on the show and putting them on the spot.

I would never do that. I went to interview Ricky Martin once and checked beforehand if there was anything he didn't want to talk about. I politely asked if he minded me asking about him being gay and coming out because I wouldn't ever want to upset anyone. He said I could ask him anything I liked and so I did and we had a great chat.

Those early days were a lot of fun and we had some amazing guests, as we always do, proper A-listers. Whoopi Goldberg came on in 2017 and she was brilliant. She just turned up with no entourage and was game for anything. She had such a great sense of humour and did everything that was asked of her. She loved *EastEnders* and re-enacted a little scene with Nadia, who of course had been in it years before.

Nadia was giving it the iconic line: 'You're not my mother!'

Whoopi was doing the Cockney accent, which was hilarious. She does the American version of *Loose*, which they call *The View*, so she just got it, and then she sat with us afterwards, chatting away for ages.

Antonio Banderas was another diamond. Because he was on the show, the night before, me and Andrea McLean had to go and watch a screening of his film *The SpongeBob Movie: Sponge Out of Water*, which was two hours of our lives we were never going to get back. But he was so handsome and he had a bacon roll with us. Obviously we weren't rude about the film to his face but it wasn't our cup of tea.

It tends to be the big stars who are the nicest. Stanley Tucci was brilliant when he was on plugging his new cookbook. We'd got my husband to make one of the recipes the night before and I'd brought it in and had to say mine was better than the one Stanley had done in the book.

The kids used to come down if there was ever someone they liked appearing on the show, so I brought Louis along the day we had Sir Ian McKellen on. Louis is a big fan of *Lord of the Rings*, so it was a real treat for him to meet Gandalf.

Sir Ian was given the dressing room next door to me, so I waited outside for him like a groupie and when he came out I said, 'Oh my God, I loved you in panto!'

'Panto?' he said.

He'd played Widow Twankey in *Aladdin* at the Old Vic in 2006 and I'd taken Louis to see it. Obviously his career has clearly been much more highbrow and prestigious than that (that was the joke) and he laughed. I introduced him to Louis and the two of them had a nice chat together.

Michael Bublé was another one who I totally loved. We were told we had fifteen minutes with him, but after half an hour we were still going strong. He was mimicking my Cockney accent and I liked him so much that I asked for a massage as I was leaving because my back was killing me. And he obliged!

When Brian Cox came on, I reminded him that we'd done a play reading together along with Angela Lansbury years before. I broke my golden rule of never asking guests for a selfie and made sure I got a picture. He's the nicest man. I loved him in *Succession* – his character Logan Roy swears even more than me!

Silly jobs

One of the *Loose Women* editors used to get me out on all these daft jobs, which I loved. They told me once that they were sending me to the Cannes Film Festival on an 'Access No Areas' ticket and I had three challenges to complete:

1. Blag my way into an A-list party
2. Get photos of myself with lots of celebrities
3. Find a yacht that we could broadcast live from on the show

It was only me, a researcher and a cameraman going out there, but I'm not afraid to ask anyone anything so I wasn't going to shy away from it. We got to Cannes and just sort of wandered around having a think about how we were going to tackle the brief ahead of the next day's edition.

I knew that if there were going to be any celebrities about, then they were likely to be at the Carlton Hotel where I'd stayed myself. So we headed over there and it proved rich pickings. We saw Michael Fassbender, Tamara Ecclestone, Harvey Weinstein (this was before #MeToo, I must add), the supermodel Erin O'Connor, who told me she was a huge *Loose Women* fan, and Robbie Williams with his wife Ayda.

I started walking up to Robbie to get a selfie with him as part of my challenge to pose for pictures with celebs when a security guard stepped towards me. I think he was about to throw me out.

Robbie told the guard, 'Leave her, she's fine', and he gave me an interview, which was really kind of him. Then I went down to the harbour where all the amazing yachts were – we're talking millions and millions of pounds' worth of boats. We walked along and I'd approach whoever was on the deck and say, 'Excuse me, my name's Linda Robson and I'm doing a show called *Loose Women*, which is live in the UK every day. Is there any chance we could film on your yacht tomorrow?'

If you don't ask, you don't get – right?

Most of them were Russian and didn't have a clue who I was or what I was on about, so they shooed us away and we kept moving, unfazed. The last yacht on the row wasn't as sparkly or as flashy as the other ones, but it was still really nice.

I saw the owner and did my 'Excuse me, my name's Linda Robson' bit and I asked him his name.

'Les,' he replied.

'Where do you live, Les?'

'Essex.'

Bingo.

'Come here, Les. I've got a favour to ask . . .'

Les was brilliant and he said yes, we could use his yacht no problem. So we headed back the next day and went live to the studio while sipping champagne. Then they showed all the clips of me hanging out with Robbie and Ayda and Michael Fassbender and it went down really, really well. I was so pleased with it!

I kept in touch with Les (that's my old habit of collecting friends wherever I go) and the following year I went back there with Mark, Louis and Bobbie Girl, getting the train to Paris and then another one on to Cannes as Mark has a fear of flying. I took them all to Les's yacht.

'Hello, we're back! And I ain't got a film crew this time!'

We watched the fireworks on his boat together and had a lovely evening.

Another time I interviewed Tom Jones where I sang to him and asked if he'd turn round for me on *The Voice* and he said, 'No chance!'

They'd given me a list of these silly quickfire questions to ask him, things like 'boxers or briefs' and 'lights on or lights off', and he took it really well so we had a good laugh about it.

I heard that some people had got the hump, but you know what? Tom had found the whole thing really funny and I'm sure he would have let me know if he hadn't.

They also sent me to watch the *Fifty Shades of Grey* film and I had to interview all the cast outside afterwards.

After I'd seen the movie, I said to the camera, 'What they've been doing in there? I've never seen anything like it. It's made me realize my husband is a lazy bleep!'

The difficult ones . . .

It hasn't always gone to plan with our celebrity guests, though.

One such episode happened when we had Kim Woodburn on the show. That's a day I won't forget anytime soon. They'd got her on with my fellow panellist Coleen Nolan because they'd appeared on *Celebrity Big Brother* together and had clashed there.

While we all felt well-prepared before going on, I was still a bit nervous, in all honesty, because she's got a reputation for being opinionated. Her and Coleen ended up disagreeing and when I tried to defend my friend, Kim criticised me too.

I was taken aback by how she reacted towards me, I didn't even know the woman.

She became increasingly frustrated while I was just sitting there, completely baffled. I was at a loss for words. This was all live on air, and I wondered if this might be something she did on purpose to get headlines, I don't know. But in any case it was an uncomfortable experience.

The disagreement escalated to the point where Kim had clearly had enough and she ended up walking off set.

We never intended for things to end like this but the situation had very quickly intensified.

And our interview with Iain Stirling, the *Love Island* narrator who's married to Laura Whitmore, was a funny one. They had just had a baby which was news in the public domain, as was their wish to keep it all quite private. I would have loved to say congratulations or to see a picture of the baby, but we respected their wishes so we didn't talk about it. If that was me, I would have wanted to tell the whole world!

Stripping off

Loose Women's Body Stories campaign in 2017 was one of the most terrifying things I've ever done. It saw us strip off to swimwear for an unairbrushed, unfiltered photo shoot aimed at celebrating real women's bodies in all their glory and was being shot by the singer Bryan Adams, who is now an acclaimed photographer, at his house in Chelsea where he has his own studio.

Not even Mark has seen me naked. I'm serious. Never, ever. I've never undressed in front of him and I've always worn granny nightdresses or pyjamas to bed. It's a self-consciousness thing, maybe because he's so fit from going to the gym all the time whereas I don't do any exercise really.

The *Loose Women* bosses were saying they would make sure we had the most beautiful and flattering swimwear to pose in, but it wasn't a project any of us were relishing. None of us were like, 'Oh my God, I can't wait to get out there and show it all off!'

I think the immediate reaction was more: 'Quick, find me a diet. I need to lose a stone in a week.'

On the day of the shoot I did *Loose Women* in the morning and then the four of us – me, Nadia Sawalha, Jane Moore and Stacey Solomon – went to the pub for a glass of wine, which was unheard of for me in the daytime. But we needed something!

We met the rest of the girls at Bryan's place where his assistants were swarming around getting the lighting all set up and the stylists had rails and rails of swimming costumes for us to try on. The good thing was we did it together. So we all walked out on to the studio floor as a group, which meant the whole experience was a lot less traumatic than it might have been.

The whole point of the shoot was that the pictures were going to be natural, so we had minimal hair and make-up, some of us had none at all. But that didn't stop Katie Price turning up wearing a full face, false eyelashes and a gallon of fake tan. That was always going to happen with her, we all knew that's just Katie. I love Katie Price but sometimes I think she deliberately tries to shock. I did an awards show with her once where we were both supposed to be presenting together but no one could find her anywhere. She eventually turned up with minutes to spare. When we got out on the stage, she started talking about herself and I had to tell her, 'Oi! It ain't about you today!'

Whenever I bump into her now, she tells me how she wants to come back to *Loose Women*. And I say, 'But, Katie, you can't f***ing behave yourself, can you?'

I do worry about her. Sometimes I thought she'd been out late the night before a show. She used to sleep in the car on her way in and would arrive in her pyjamas and get dressed when she got there. I used to think that was quite a good idea actually!

She always made plenty of headlines whenever she was on, though. And I've seen the other side of her with her son Harvey, who she has loved and fought for his whole life. We were on another shoot together once and she brought him along because he had a hospital appointment afterwards. He seemed quite happy sitting with his laptop when he suddenly sprang up in a rage and kicked the table in the air, sending the computer flying.

Katie defused it immediately. 'Look at me, Harvey! Look at me. That was unacceptable.'

And he said, 'Sorry, Mum,' and quietly sat back down again.

I thought that was amazing. The connection and understanding she has with Harvey is all credit to her because caring for him is not easy.

Back at the Body Stories shoot, Bryan was so good at putting us at ease. He said to just do what we wanted to do, keeping it natural, and the atmosphere in the studio was really laid-back, which helped. He told us afterwards that he thought we'd been brilliant and brave and he'd really enjoyed the day.

A few weeks later, me and Stacey had to go down to Westfield where they unveiled the billboard – a big moment. We spoke to women out shopping and asked what they thought of it and everyone was really positive. And then the whole thing sort of exploded and we had women all over the country sharing pictures of their natural bodies, which felt really empowering. I've got our framed picture up in my kitchen and I absolutely love it.

We recreated the campaign four years later, this time showing the before and after of an image which had gone through one of those body-tuning apps people use on social media. I found that one a bit more awkward because we were all shot individually in front of the crew we work with every day. My response to embarrassment is to turn everything into a joke, so that's what I did to get through it.

By then Frankie Bridge was on the show and, although she's lovely, no one wanted to stand next to her! She's so beautiful that her photoshopped image looked hardly any different to the natural one. Frankie's been a good addition to the show and has opened us out to a younger audience. Since she's only in her early thirties she has a different take on a lot of things, and it's been a really interesting dynamic.

All in all, I think those campaigns were definitely worth the discomfort and I'm pleased we did them. I won't say yes to everything, though. Once the bosses asked us – and this is God's honest truth – to go and get a vagina mould done as we were exploring the very serious topic of vagina dysmorphia and raising awareness about gynaecological cancers.

And I can understand why they asked, but for me this was a step too far.

Live and Loose

In the autumn of 2023, we took *Loose Women* on tour to perform the show live in theatres across the country and I can honestly say it was the most fun I'd had in years.

I loved every minute of it.

I did eleven out of the sixteen shows and was gutted when it came to an end – we had such a blast. When we came out on the stage at the London Palladium, I felt like I was in the Spice Girls!

I was wracked with nerves before my first show. I'm used to live theatre and it doesn't faze me, but that's when I've got a set script to follow every night. This was a bit more free-wheeling and unpredictable and none of us really knew what to expect. And there were a couple of times when even I was lost for words like the night a woman in the audience revealed that the strangest place she'd had sex was on a tractor.

I presume it wasn't moving at the time.

There was also the day me and Charlene travelled up to Newcastle together and I managed to take us to the wrong theatre. We nearly ended up in the *SpongeBob SquarePants* musical by mistake.

We were supposed to be at the City Hall (not the Theatre Royal), and we had to leg it across Newcastle to get there on time. Charlene said she was never trusting me again after that.

The audiences were amazing and we felt so much love from them. Crowds of them would wait outside the stage door after every show and stopping for a chat and a sign with them was one of the best things about being on tour.

My backstage rider was very basic, just a cheese and pickle sandwich and a pot of tea. I'm not a prima donna.

Each night just before we went on stage, I'd make the

other women and the crew stand in a huddle and do a pelvic thrust. It's what we used to do on *Birds of a Feather* before we went out in front of the studio audience and it became just as much of a team-bonding ritual with the *Loose* lot.

We were already a tight-knit unit but life on the road definitely brought us all closer together. Me and Denise had such a laugh and got to know each other really well and there was one night me and Kelly ended up in bed at our hotel watching *Family Guy* at 1 a.m. while ordering room service. Rock and roll!

I can't pick and choose my favourite show, but I did love being at the Palladium. I wasn't even on the panel that day, but they asked me to go along and when I came out the audience went mad! They were chanting: 'Linda! Linda! Linda!' – my kids were there and they said: 'It was like you were Madonna, Mum!'

This was a stage where Frank Sinatra and Shirley Bassey had performed live. All the greats. All that history and culture.

And now, here were the Loose Women belting out 'That's What Friends Are For' at the top of our voices. Mostly in tune.

Life's hilarious sometimes, isn't it?

Friendships and feuds?

I've always got on with everyone at *Loose* but there are naturally going to be people who you gel with better than others. There's never been anyone I've refused to sit on the panel with, although I can't speak for others on the show in the past. No, I'm not mentioning any names!

And I think a couple of people have taken against me for whatever reason. I remember going into the canteen once and seeing someone from the panel sitting there with another woman. As I was walking towards her, I could see she was doing this thing of talking behind her hand and looking at me at the same time. Subtle as a brick.

Lauren was with me and she said, 'She doesn't like you, does she, Mum?'

'I'm not sure, Lauren . . .'

'No, I really don't think she does.'

As we reached her table, she suddenly broke off from whispering and was all gushy saying, 'Oh, hiiiii, Linda! How are you?', which just felt really fake.

This was when I was starting out as a regular and I don't know if certain people were feeling insecure because they were bringing new panellists in. Maybe she felt like she was going to be given the boot. And thinking about it, she didn't last much longer! That had nothing to do with me, though. I don't think any of us can presume we're safe for ever.

A lot of the supposed 'spats' are whipped up by the press and we're all used to that by now, but there was an incident which got a huge amount of publicity and left us all quite confused. And some of us very upset indeed.

When Saira Khan quit unexpectedly in January 2021,

she did not go quietly. It wasn't so much the fact that Saira Khan quit *Loose Women* as the manner in which she did it. If she'd wanted to leave the show, that was her choice, but she made some comments about going which we were all taken aback by. In interviews she had a lot to say about the show and the people she'd worked with, which I'd found surprising. That wasn't the *Loose Women* I knew.

I've always had a good relationship with Saira and we'd socialized together with my grandkids and her kids, so I found it all really mystifying. I wasn't sure if any of it was aimed at me, but I'd like to think not. I did wonder if it had anything to do with her agent, though. At one point I knew quite a few people who were represented by that particular agent, but one by one they've parted ways. The agent once asked me whether I would have any interest in going on her books.

And, well, let's just say I politely declined.

Anyway, Saira suddenly unfollowed some of us on social media and carried on making these cryptic comments about people she didn't like, and it all felt really unnecessary and uncalled for. I think it's sad that she left and that it happened in the way that it did, because I thought Saira was a great panellist and I can't understand what motivated it. Having said that, I don't feel any animosity towards her and we're still in touch over Instagram, inasmuch as if she puts photos up of the kids, I'll 'like' them. I can just about manage 'liking' photos but that's as tech savvy as I get!

But while there have been highs and lows and it's not

always been sunshine and flowers, I couldn't ever be without my work family. Signing that permanent contract just over a decade ago was the start of a wonderful new chapter and the team has been right by my side both on and off screen as the most supportive group of friends you could wish for.

Me and My Baggy Mouth

Loose lips

When I die, I'll have it written on my tombstone: HERE LIES BAGGY MOUTH. SHE JUST COULDN'T KEEP IT SHUT.

I don't know who came up with the nickname, but I'll hold my hands up and say it's fully deserved. I can't be trusted with a secret because without meaning to I blurt it out before I realize what I'm saying. My mouth starts moving before my brain has engaged. I'll say things like, 'Oh that's a great fancy dress costume they've made you wear' when it's the person's actual clothes. That happens to me all the time but it's always innocently done.

And I'm constantly in trouble from the family for saying too much. Something will pop into my head and I say it on live telly, forgetting there are people all over the country watching. Like the time I revealed me and Mark had broken the bed getting frisky the previous night, which the newspapers had a field day with.

I once told everyone that Mark got his back and chest waxed and one of our dustmen saw him in the street the next day and said, 'What's all this about you and the waxing?'

When I got home later, Mark said, 'What the hell have you been saying now on *Loose Women*?'

I suppose I'm one of those people who loves a good

chat – I'll happily talk to anyone and enjoy conversation so much that I forget to filter what I say. I'll also pour my heart out to complete strangers. I'll be sat on a plane and by the time we get off the person sitting next to me will know my life story and I'll know theirs and all.

The kids are always going, 'Mum! Why are you telling people about your private business?' But I can't help it. I'm just me and I can't be anything else. Unfortunately 'me' sometimes gets me into trouble.

Just slipped out

The worst one was in October 2021 when I honestly thought it was curtains for me. I was genuinely frightened that I was going to get sacked.

In real life I admit I eff and jeff a fair bit, so I do have to tone my fruitier language down for daytime ITV. OK, right down. However, the odd 'arse' slips out occasionally and I've had to say sorry straight away in case anyone gets offended and complains.

I wasn't actually on the *Loose Women* panel on the day in question, but they'd asked me to come in and intro-duce a competition to win £1 million, and part of that involved me wheeling on the safe full of cash as a prop. As far as I knew (and this is absolutely true), it was a rehearsal. Anyway, this safe thing was heavy and I had to push it on to the set with two security guards flank-ing me.

Before we went on, I'd been mucking about with the guards, picking up the money and stuffing it down my shirt, and we'd all been laughing, so I was probably more relaxed than I would have been otherwise. When it came to walking on to where Charlene White and panellists Brenda Edwards, Sunetra Sarker and Kelle Bryan were sitting behind the desk, the camera was in front of me as I was saying my lines straight down the lens.

'One million pounds!' I said. 'Right here in this trolley. It came straight from the ITV bank account this morn—'

But then, without warning, the camera kind of moved higher up and swooped slightly behind me so I didn't have a clue where I was supposed to be looking. I broke off from the script.

'How the f*** do I look at it?' I asked.

The girls collectively drew breath and I knew what I'd done.

'Are we live on air?' I asked, panicking.

The studio suddenly felt like it was spinning and I wished the ground would open up and swallow me whole.

I could hear the *Loose Women* anchor Charlene White apologizing profusely and saying, 'Linda knows she's done wrong', and I was vaguely aware of the audience gasping and giggling in shock.

My heart was in my mouth and I felt physically ill. *Oh God*, I thought. *I've done it this time. I'm definitely going to be out of a job.*

Charlene, bless her, saved my life. She's saved my life many times to be honest, but this was the most serious. She immediately apologized on my behalf while I ploughed on with the rest of my script, not knowing what else to do. I was shaking. Brenda was crippled over laughing behind me.

I was still trembling when I came off, thinking, *That's it. I've blown it.*

I went back into the green room and all the producers were huddled in a corner, deep in conversation – I knew exactly what they were discussing and I could feel my face burning up. They saw me and said they didn't think I should go back on for part two. It was half-term as well so there would have been loads of kids watching at home.

Andi Peters happened to be there because he'd been doing *This Morning* just before us and he chipped in and said if I didn't go back on, everyone would think I'd been sent home in disgrace. The best thing to do, he said, would be to front it out and make a joke of it. So he went on with me after the break and he brought some soap with him and said he was going to wash my mouth out, which made everything feel a bit lighter.

I went over to meet Bobbie Girl at Westfield afterwards and she said, 'Mum, what have you done?'

The kids told me I'd gone viral. I remember I was getting on a train a couple of days later and there were a load of Newcastle United fans who were down for a football match and they were all calling me a legend. But I was terrified that I was going to lose my job because this time I'd crossed a line.

In the end I did get a dressing-down, but they recognized it was an honest mistake. They actually didn't get a single complaint about it, so I think the viewers at home realized it was a slip of the tongue. Although I've never been asked to host a *Loose* competition since. Funny that.

A pronoun pickle

Transwoman Caitlyn Jenner (who used to be Bruce) caused a bit of a nightmare for me when she came on *Loose Women* in 2017. She was over here promoting something or other and I had to drum it into myself to use the right pronouns.

'She, Linda. She, she, she.'

I promised myself I wouldn't forget.

It was me and Jane Moore doing the interview and the gallery was in my ear the whole time repeating 'she, she, she' so I wouldn't muck it up.

Caitlyn was really honest and I thoroughly enjoyed talking to her. I was also relieved to have got through the interview without putting my foot in it.

And then her PR came over and said they had to go and, after all my efforts, I screwed it up. 'He don't wanna go – he's enjoying himself!' I said.

Argh! I think it was the fact the pressure was finally off and I just unravelled. Thank goodness Caitlyn herself was fine about it.

Covid controversy

I accidentally kicked off a bit of controversy on our first show back in January 2021 following the Christmas holiday. We were all talking about our Christmas days and how we'd spent them and I said we'd had Lauren and

Steve and the girls over for dinner because they go to their nanny Brenda's on Boxing Day.

Lauren and Steve were in our bubble for childcare and so I thought it was OK, but apparently the government rules on Covid at the time said otherwise and people watching were furious with me. They were phoning in to ITV and messaging me on social media saying I should lose my job.

People were going on, saying just because I was on the telly didn't mean that I didn't have to stick to the same rules as everyone else. That is not something I've ever thought for one second. I've never thought I was better than anyone. And I didn't want anyone to think I'd not taken Covid seriously. We really did – Mark even volunteered at a Covid vaccine centre so he could do his bit. The children's bookshop he'd run for several years on Chadwell Street was forced to close during lockdown and we had to let it go in the end, so we were personally and financially affected by what was happening. And it had nearly killed me not seeing the family.

I felt that I shouldn't come in for a week after that so I could lie low and let it die down. I was a bit upset about having to hide away, but I think it was the right thing to do because the chatter did go away after a few days when the Twitter mob moved on to the next thing to get angry about.

Mark was so worried about getting Covid and tested himself regularly. When I tested positive during the first wave, I felt as if he wanted me to move into a hotel.

The kids were horrified at the thought of me being by myself. 'We couldn't leave Mummy on her own when she has Covid!' they said to him.

He ended up staying put, but, Jesus, he did his whole Dr Kildare routine whenever he had to come within a few metres of me, putting his rubber gloves and mask on to deliver my tray of food before scuttling off again, probably to hose himself down.

He's always been careful to avoid catching any bugs but he took it to another level with Covid. He actually managed to dodge getting it until July 2022, so he was obviously doing something right. By that time I don't think I knew anyone who hadn't had it, so Mark had been the last man standing.

I couldn't wait to have my vaccine; I was straight down there for my appointment as soon as I got the call. To me it was a huge relief that we finally had a way out of this nightmare and I was delighted to take it. I never suffered any side effects from it and I'm up to date with all my boosters too. Not everyone in the family has had it, though, and it's not something we can really talk about any more because it causes too much grief. I love them all dearly but we are never going to agree on it.

Whoops, I did it again

It's the times when I'm trying my hardest to self-censor that are the most dangerous. When me and Lesley won *Celebrity Coach Trip*, we weren't allowed to tell anyone about it because there were several months before the show was going to be on TV. Can you imagine how difficult that was for me?

I was so stressed about keeping it a secret because I knew deep down it was only a matter of time before I put my foot right in it. That happened in spectacular style when I was talking about it as part of the promotion on *Loose Women* and accidentally revealed we'd won.

I had the producers in my ear saying, 'Spoiler, spoiler! You're not supposed to say that – you're going to be in trouble now!'

Me and my mouth. Again!

So then I had to hastily backtrack and pretend I was referring to winning one of the challenges rather than the show itself. I don't think that washed with people watching, though.

It's too late for me now. This is how I am. I'll never learn.

Campmates and Cannabis

Welcome to the jungle

In between the *Birds* theatre tours, I'd signed up to *I'm a Celebrity . . . Get Me Out of Here!* thinking it was now or never. I'd always turned it down in the past but it's such an iconic show and something inside told me this might be my last chance. It was 2012 and I'd not long lost my mum, so it was possibly a bit of a reaction to that as well. Anyway, I said yes.

All campmates had to keep the fact we were taking part a big secret, which you'll probably have realized by now is not something I'm particularly good at. I told Lauren and Bobbie Girl and they were so excited for me. They reckoned I'd do brilliantly in there because they knew I'd never be horrible to anyone or get involved in any rows and that I'd give everything a good go. But I managed to keep it from Louis and Mark until about two days before I left for Australia, which was an achievement, especially for me.

We all went out to dinner and I told them what was happening. Their reaction was very different to how the girls had been. Mark said, 'Oh God, Linda. You're going to be the first person to kill yourself during a challenge on live TV.'

And Louis was worried too. 'I don't think you should do it, Mum.'

'Well, I am doing it and I'm leaving in forty-eight hours,' I said.

'How will we know if you're all right?' asked Louis.

He wasn't trying to put a dampener on things; he was genuinely concerned. That's when Bobbie Girl came up with the idea of me touching my ear whenever Ant and Dec came into camp and we went live so everyone knew I was OK and was thinking about them. I did that every night until I was voted out. And Lauren suggested making a squawking noise as another way of communicating with them back home, so whenever I could I'd go, 'Coo coo! Coo coo!' like a wild bird. It actually caught on, and Ant and Dec were doing it too by the end.

Illicit phone calls

It was a tightly run operation in Australia. Crystal was the member of the production team who was assigned to look after me when I arrived and her main job was to make sure I didn't bump into any of the other celebrities. They wanted whoever else was taking part to be a surprise so that when we were all introduced on camera the reactions and first impressions would be real.

If you wanted to leave your hotel room, all the producers had to radio each other to check the coast was clear. And you weren't allowed to call home either, because by now the line-up had been announced to the public and they didn't want your family spilling the beans.

I got Crystal a bit tipsy one night and I was begging her for a borrow of her phone to call Mark and the kids, but she said I wasn't allowed. She was in the room next door to me and the idea was that she could hear me if I left, but I think she was in a fairly deep sleep so I managed to sneak out with a hoodie on and walked out of the hotel.

All the staff had been told not to give us an outside telephone line, so I had no option but to leave the complex. I went to a phone box and did a reverse-charge call to my landline back in London. Bobbie Girl picked up and I told her not to worry about me. I was all right and would be heading into the jungle the next day. And she told me every single person who was going in there with me because it had been in all the papers. After that, I went back to the hotel and no one ever found out about my secret mission! I suppose they'll know after reading it here . . .

My campmates were the boxer David Haye, Charlie Brooks from *EastEnders*, Pussycat Doll Ashley Roberts, the former darts player Eric Bristow, *Corrie* star Helen Flanagan, Tory MP Nadine Dorries, *Dr Who* actor Colin Baker, eighties singer Limahl, comedian Brian Conley, Hugo Taylor from *Made in Chelsea* and the chef Rosemary Shrager. I got on well with all of them. The only one I used to row a bit with was Eric, who I'd known when we were younger and used to go to the same club. He could be really rude, like he'd tell me I needed to stay in the jungle for as long as possible because I had to lose weight. I could give it back, though, and I'd tell him at least I hadn't been hit with the ugly stick.

We kept in touch afterwards but our text messages would normally just be a string of insults. I messaged him once to let him know my son-in-law Steve was coming down to the darts at Alexandra Palace and could he come and say hello and look after him a bit. Eric said yes that would be fine, but when Steve got there and said hello, Eric looked at him and snapped, 'What do you want?'

I texted him the next day, saying, *You're a rude vile pig, Eric Bristow.*

And then he died, so that turned out to be the last message I sent him. I felt a bit bad about that, but it was our sense of humour and in keeping with the tone of our relationship as a whole. And besides, I hadn't said anything that wasn't true.

My campmates

I loved Charlie Brooks – what a lovely woman. But the show was heavily criticized when they brought in her daughter Kiki, who was only seven at the time, to be part of a game. It involved Charlie having to choose a door to open which would reveal a mystery prize, but she chose the wrong one and came away with nothing. She didn't realize that Kiki had been behind one of them as the 'prize' until later on. Kiki was crying and Charlie was distraught thinking about how excited her little girl would have been to see her mummy. It was really cruel and I think they got into trouble for that because there were so many complaints.

I really got on with Rosemary Shrager and Nadine Dorries as well, and we kept in touch. I went to meet Nadine a few times for lunch afterwards at the House of Commons.

Here's some gossip for you: David Haye had a phone with him which he'd managed to smuggle in. He'd handed over one phone when he got there but hadn't told them he had a second one with him which he'd been using to call and text family at home before we went in. He got it all the way into camp – the producers might have known, but who was going to be brave enough to ask David Haye to give it up? I think it was after the first night that our team Croc Creek had spent in the luxury camp that a producer very politely asked him to hand it over and he reluctantly agreed.

Brian Conley only lasted nine days before he left for medical reasons. He'd stopped taking the medication for his depression and he'd been behaving out of character. I don't think they showed most of what was going on, but the whole cast was growing increasingly concerned about his behaviour. Then one day he went into the Bush Telegraph and never came out again. We were all asking where Brian was, but they'd taken him away, and I think he went to hospital because he was in such a bad way. They had no choice but to take him out. His wife and daughter had arrived in Australia that day, so it was good that they were there for him.

Brian's actually a very nice man, and I went to see him in panto back in the UK a few weeks later and he seemed fine again. I just think he put a lot of pressure on himself with that show and coupled with him stopping taking his meds it created this big old mess.

Big-money offers

We lived off rice and beans because Helen Flanagan was so hopeless at the Bushtucker Trials and never won any stars for meals. The public kept on voting her to do them precisely because of that and it became a running joke for people watching back home.

It wasn't a joke for us, though! Having said that, I looked gorgeous when I came out of there. I'd lost about two stone, and my skin and hair were lovely. Even on the rare occasion we were given something a bit more substantial than rice and beans, I hadn't really eaten it. One day they gave us possum sausages. I asked everyone what exactly a possum was, just as this big rat thing ran past us in the camp.

'That's one,' they all said.

So there was no way I was eating that.

But I did everything that was asked of me, just as I'd said I would. I did challenges with critters all over me and was suspended on a high wire above a fifty-metre drop and generally really enjoyed myself. Nevertheless, I was quite pleased when I was the third one to be voted out. Once you'd been eliminated, you could either lock yourself in your hotel room and get thirty grand for doing an exclusive interview with a newspaper or you could go out and about with your family and have a nice time together.

So I said, no, I didn't want the money. Louis, Bobbie Girl, Lauren, Steve and Lila had all flown out and Kiffy Swash was there as well because Joe was hosting the spin-off show on ITV2.

The kids had already run me up a nice bill by the time I got there. To top it off, I had also paid for the whole family to fly out business class, which meant my fee was more or less swallowed up by the time they touched down. But I knew I was doing another tour of *Birds of a*

Feather when I came out, so I wasn't going into it hoping I might get a job out of it. And, let's face it, you're not going to get a lucrative or respected acting gig off the back of doing *I'm a Celebrity*.

Me and Biggins go potty

In 2017 I got the strangest job offer of my career so far. It was for a three-part ITV show called *Gone to Pot: American Road Trip*, which would see a group of midlifer celebs travel across California by bus, sampling various forms of marijuana and exploring the legalization of it.

My agent said not to do it. She said, 'As a face of ITV Daytime, you will never work again if you're on telly smoking weed.'

My kids, on the other hand, were like, 'Yeah, go for it!' They said it would make me such a cool mum.

I thought it sounded like a really fascinating show and I've always been interested in how marijuana can work medicinally. Some years before, I'd become Twitter friends with a boy called Darren Blackwood who had leukaemia and another really rare form of cancer, which gave him something like a one in eight billion chance of survival. He started taking cannabis, which his mum had got for him, and he's still alive years later. The last time I spoke to him he was working as a chef for Heston Blumenthal and his family are convinced he's survived this long because of the cannabis. At one stage I'd even gone to the hospice in Bristol to say goodbye to him, so for him to come back from that makes me think there's something in it.

I'd never taken it myself. I told you earlier how me and Pauline were never offered drugs or, to our knowledge, were even ever around them. If we were, we were oblivious to it. I'm not naive and I know that a lot of it goes on in the industry, especially with the younger ones who get thrust into the limelight and invited to all these different showbiz parties. Me and Pauline really only ever went to Stringfellows.

Anyway, I said I'd do the show because I fancied a little adventure. I know ITV were nervous about it because they'd never done anything like it before. I remember the director, Kevin Mundye, saying to me, 'You know this is going to go mad overnight? Everyone's going to be talking about it . . .'

And it did blow up. Where else are you going to find Linda Robson, Christopher Biggins, *EastEnders'* Pam St Clement, the former professional darts player Bobby George and ex-footballer John Fashanu smoking pot and getting stoned together every night? Oh my God, it was one of my best jobs ever – three of the most fun weeks of my life.

It's a bit weird to think my and Pam St Clement's paths hadn't crossed before this show, but we'd never met, and to be honest I didn't think I was going to like her. I suppose I thought she'd be like her *EastEnders* character Pat Butcher, all hard-faced and hot-tempered, but she couldn't have been lovelier. So well spoken too.

Biggins I'd known for years and he's one of my favourite people. So is his partner Neil, who is the sweetest man. Biggins tells a good story and there's no one better at holding court, but he doesn't half name-drop.

I'll sit there counting them. 'Oh, there's the first one. And another. That's three and four there . . . Shall I pick them up for you, Chris?' as he mentions Joan Collins, Barbara Windsor and everyone else.

He loves his art and the walls of his house are covered in paintings. When I was there for dinner once, I said, 'You're getting on now, aren't you? Who are you leaving all these lovely paintings to when you're gone?' And I went round and put stickers on his David Hockney originals. 'I'll have that one here, and that one over there. Ooh, I love this one . . .'

The next time I saw him, he'd bought me a Hockney painting tote bag. 'There's your f***ing Hockney,' he said.

Everyone loves him. I've never heard anyone say a bad word about Biggins. He's always so dapper in his Hawaiian shirts and he's the best company. I keep telling him that he needs to get a stairlift put in that house of his, though. It's three storeys and I have no idea how he manages. I think Neil probably has to push his arse up the stairs.

Out of Fash-ion

To put it politely, Bobby George and John Fashanu didn't hit it off on *Gone to Pot*. It all got a bit tense at times because Bobby was taking the piss and John isn't the sort of person who likes having the piss taken out of him. I had to tell Bobby to tone it down a bit.

There was no harm in John; he was just a bit sad really.

He's a very serious person and I know he's had a lot of troubles in his life, so that might explain it. He was the only one who didn't try cannabis. He was dead against it. I think that's maybe why he was on the show, to act as the dissenting voice. The rest of us tried everything we were offered, maybe we tried a bit too much. Biggins threw up the first time he took it.

We all went to this Puff, Pass and Paint class where we all had to paint a picture of a cactus and have a bong and that was great fun. There was a serious side to the series, though, and we went to see this little girl who had been having several seizures a day and couldn't speak or communicate. When she started taking medical marijuana, gradually the fitting slowed down and, although it hadn't stopped completely, she was so much better than she had been before.

John got really upset that day. He's got a son with special needs and he said he wished he'd known more about the benefits of cannabis when his boy was younger, so I think he had changed his mind a bit by the end.

We were all asked on the final show if any of us thought it should be legalized in the UK and me, Pam, Biggins and Bobby put our hands up and John kind of waved his in the middle. Medicinally I think it can do wonders. Anyone I know who has anything wrong with them, I always suggest they try cannabis.

Me? I enjoyed it. It made me giggly and relaxed and it helped with my sleep too. I have to be careful, though, because I have an addictive personality and it could get me into trouble.

While we were filming in California, I went to see Robbie and Ayda Williams, who were living in LA at the time.

I'd got to know Ayda through *Loose Women* when she'd joined the panel the year before. We were all a bit in awe of her at *Loose* because she'd arrive with a big entourage of hair, make-up and stylists bringing pieces from Gucci and Valentino. I love all that because you get an insight into how the other half live, and Ayda was never horrible with it. She was lovely and she was a good Loose Woman – we loved her on the show. And they got a double whammy because Robbie came on loads of times as well.

So Ayda got in touch and said she'd heard I was in town and to come down to the house for a cuppa. I bought some petrol-station flowers and got an Uber to their place in Beverly Hills 90210 that was behind these huge gates.

It was amazing. The kids were there playing in this silver caravan in the garden and there was someone pre-paring food for us. As you went into the main entrance there was a massive bronze horse, but none of it was over the top like *The Real Housewives of Beverly Hills*; it was all tastefully done out. Just beautiful.

Robbie took me around and showed me everything, and me and him got on really well. We're both from simi-lar working-class backgrounds, although obviously I don't have a house in 90210. I told them all about *Gone to Pot* and Robbie said I should have brought Biggins with me.

When I got back and told Biggins that, he went mad. 'Well, you should have asked me to be your f***ing plus one!' he cried. That would have given him some excellent name-dropping opportunities. He'd have dined out all year on that one.

Prank calls

One evening after filming, me and Biggins were in his hotel room watching telly and my phone bleeped with a text. I opened it and it said one word: *C****.

I was shocked.

'Chris,' I said, 'someone's just texted me and called me a c***.'

'Noooooooooo!' he said, equally horrified. 'Call them back, Linda, and give them what for.'

So I dialled the number and his phone started ringing . . .

He's been in my phone as Chris C*** ever since. Meant in the nicest possible way.

Biggins was a very comforting presence for me on that trip. I don't think he knows even now how much. Because although I had a great time out in the States, there was a fair bit going on beneath the surface. Things I was trying to hide but which were simmering away and becoming increasingly difficult to keep a lid on.

I'd always enjoyed a glass of wine, but by 2017 this had escalated to a bottle a night. I was supposed to have given it up as part of a sugar-free diet *Loose Women* had put me on as a feature on the show, but shortly before we went away to film *Gone to Pot*, I'd started drinking again and was doing it in secret.

While we were out there, I'd buy those quarter bottles of vodka and drink them on my own in my hotel room at night to knock myself out. I was still functioning perfectly well and was able to get up in the morning as fresh as a daisy and work without feeling any effects, so I told myself it wasn't an issue. But this was on top of sleeping tablets, which I'd been taking on and off for about eighteen years – ever since I'd gone to Australia for *A Passionate Woman* and a doctor had recommended them as a way of beating the jet lag.

It was all forming part of a very dangerous pattern. I thought I had things under control, but over the next year my grip on everything grew weaker and I was headed for a breakdown. A breakdown which would see me forced to quit work, check into rehab and be put on suicide watch.

Rock Bottom

The last person you'd expect

Before I experienced it myself and the devastating impact it had on my family, I was quite ignorant about mental health issues. I'd had friends and close relatives go through battles with depression and anxiety and I knew it was hellish for them, but I really had no level of understanding, and part of me used to think people should try pulling themselves together and getting on with it.

What happened to me I would never have thought possible. Not me, Linda Robson. I was one of life's strong people. I soldiered on no matter what. Whatever the world threw at me, I could cope with it. I'd always been the one to look after others. I was the least likely candidate for a breakdown.

But if there's one thing I've learned over the last few turbulent years, it's that mental health issues don't discriminate and they have nothing to do with how 'strong' you are. If it can happen to me, it can happen to anyone, and I hope that sharing my experience might help someone who is experiencing similar problems. Because I wouldn't wish any of this on my worst enemy.

I've thought about it a lot and what might have triggered my illness, but I don't think it was ever one thing. Although the final descent into suicidal despair was frighteningly quick, there had been a series of events in my life building up over a number of years and possibly dating back to the anxiety I began to suffer after Ben Kinsella's murder. It was mainly around the safety of my own children, and perhaps if I'd got help for it at the time, rather than allowing it to fester, then things might have turned out differently.

Then there was my alcohol and sleeping pill use, which I'd deluded myself for years into thinking was fine because it cured my insomnia. But there's no planet where drinking a bottle of wine a night is 'fine', and that level of alcohol consumption is always going to come and eat you up eventually. And I've always had OCD, more than just liking my house to be spick and span. I think it was initially learned behaviour from my mum, who was a bit like that, but I always managed to stop it from becoming too much of an issue. It was only when everything else started to implode that the OCD went into overdrive.

The real deterioration started with an episode of *Loose Women* in January 2017, when they showed me the calories and sugar I was having with my bottle of wine a night, and it was the equivalent to something ridiculous like a hundred doughnuts across a month.

I found that really shocking, because you don't think of wine as being fattening, do you? But I had gained a lot of weight and was keen to do something about it because I was worried about diabetes and all the other conditions which can develop when you're bigger than you should be.

The producers had asked me if I would go on a sugar-free diet and they would follow my progress on the show. They said they'd get me a dietician, monitor everything, and we'd do some sort of big reveal when I'd lost the weight. So I stopped drinking my bottle of wine that very night; I effectively went cold turkey. Ruth Langsford had suggested replacing it with elderflower water but I wasn't keen on that, so I'd make myself smoothies and cups of tea at 10 p.m., which was the time I'd usually be breaking out the booze.

There was a major problem with the new regime, though. I found I wasn't able to sleep, and so to combat the insomnia I upped my zopiclone sleeping tablets to one and a half every night.

I went to the GP to try and get some more sleeping pills but she refused me and instead prescribed diazepam, which she said would help me come off the zopiclone, calm me down and get me to sleep.

Mark hated it because he said I was now in a situation where I was taking more drugs than ever, and unfortunately I had a really bad reaction to the diazepam and instead of calming me down it sent me doolally. I was hyper all the time and my OCD was another level. I was having five baths a day and constantly washing the bed-clothes. As soon as the bin had been emptied, I'd have to change it again, even if there was only a teabag in it.

After stopping drinking the wine, I went down to a size eight and everyone was telling me how good I looked because of the weight loss, but inside I was falling apart. I fought so hard to keep hidden from friends and family just how bad things were, and that in itself was exhausting.

Desperate for a solution to the way I was feeling, I went back to drinking, hoping to find some peace there. Over the next few months, the booze became more of a problem. I drank until I passed out – as I sank into what

I now know was a deep depression, passing out was exactly what I wanted. I didn't want to get through the rest of the day.

Out of control

We used to go for lunch at the Vineyard on Islington's Upper Street where I would say to the family that I was going to the toilet and then secretly ask for two glasses of white wine at the bar on my way there. I'd neck them both and then go to the loo. Then on my way back I'd order another two glasses and neck them as well before going back to the table, having downed the best part of a bottle of wine in the space of a few minutes.

I started taking my toothbrush and toothpaste with me everywhere, which was partly to do with my OCD but also to try and disguise the smell of alcohol on my breath. Mark and the kids would ask why I'd brought my toothbrush out and I'd get nasty with them. 'What? I can't even bring my toothbrush out without being interrogated?' So the pressure I was putting myself under was making me snappy and irritable with the people I loved. I hated that.

I used to eat oranges to cover up the smell of alcohol but I don't think it worked. I now know it's almost impossible to disguise, and the girls at *Loose Women* must have smelled it on me when I got into the make-up chair because I can smell it on people now. We had a guest on the show not that long ago who I won't name, but I knew straight away they had been drinking before they came on.

You can't kid a kidder.

The Loose Women intervention

It was always going to reach a crisis point, and everything came to a head while I was away on a break with some of the girls from the show in Ibiza in July 2018. It was an annual trip for me and the girls and we'd been three years on the trot, although the bosses hated it because it meant there was hardly anyone available for work.

I'd taken vodka in my case which I'd drink alone in my room. I never drank alcohol in front of the others because I was still trying to disguise how bad things were. But my OCD was completely out of hand and I couldn't disguise that because I was in a terrible state over there. I had to have my phone charged at one hundred per cent all the time otherwise I'd go into a fluster that the battery would run down and the kids wouldn't be able to contact me. So I'd take those portable chargers everywhere and if the phone went down even to ninety-six per cent I'd start panicking and have to plug it in, unable to settle until it was back to being fully charged again.

In previous years we'd been up on the tables dancing and having a great time, but I wasn't enjoying myself on this trip at all. The girls were worried and they confronted me in my bedroom one night and told me so.

'You're not right, Linda,' said Nadia, who took the lead. 'Something is really wrong and we think you need help.'

I agreed and for the first time admitted that I couldn't cope.

Nadia said later it was like my dimmer switch was fading and they had actually thought it might be the start of dementia. She was the one who said I had to get to the Priory – she had a friend who had been in there and the treatment had been brilliant.

I knew the girls were right, but I felt like I'd ruined their holiday. They shouldn't have had to look after me; they should have been out there having a whale of a time. But instead they were having to stay with me while I was getting more and more agitated and distressed.

Nadia phoned Mark and Lauren at home and told them what was happening, and Stacey said she would take me straight to the Priory, booking us both on a flight back to the UK a day earlier than planned.

I was in bits all the way back – I couldn't even talk – but Stacey was amazing at helping me stay composed, on the surface at least. I played a game on her phone and as soon as we got off the plane, she got us a taxi and we headed directly to the Priory. Mark, Lauren, Bobbie Girl and Louis were there waiting for us when we arrived. But within a few minutes of getting there, we noticed some-one taking pictures of me. Obviously that's against the rules, but clearly no one was enforcing them at that moment and it freaked me out enough for Mark to say he wasn't leaving me there and we'd find somewhere else.

They took me home and straight away found me a place at another clinic. I knew I needed to get there as quickly as possible – I'd got to the point where I didn't want to stay at home because I'd have found a way to drink. I needed to be put somewhere I didn't have any access to alcohol.

Mark drove me up there the next day and I stayed for six weeks, but it was the most depressed I've ever been and I never even saw a doctor face to face in all that time. I had a Skype call with one and the only worthwhile thing he did was prescribe me more diazepam. So it was a total waste of time in my opinion.

They only let you have your phone for half an hour a night and I missed the family so much that it physically ached. Mark would come with the kids to visit me every Sunday and those visits felt like the only thing I was living for. But at the same time part of me would dread them coming because I knew I would have to say goodbye to them again and that would leave me feeling even worse.

I also felt terrible that I was ruining their Sundays, which had always been such special family days for us, spent together over a delicious home-cooked roast. Now they were forced to slog halfway across the country to visit me in this cold, sterile clinic.

After the six weeks were up, I came home but things were as bad as they'd ever been. I was scared to come home because I knew I was still unwell and was guaranteed to start drinking again. I hadn't had a drink in all the time I'd been at the clinic, but now I was more than making up for that and downing whatever I could get my hands on.

Self-destruction

I went back to work at *Loose Women* where I managed to keep how bad things were at home under wraps by willing myself to hold it together for long enough to get through the show. Then I'd revert to self-destruct mode as soon as I was finished.

I'd come out of filming and on the way home I'd ask the driver to stop so I could pop out and get a little bottle of vodka which I'd get into bed with and drink until I passed out.

My family had to go round to our local shop and tell the man he wasn't to serve me alcohol any more. So I started going to a shop a bit further away where they didn't know me and in the end Mark and the kids had to start locking me in the house, which was the only way to stop me. We have wrought-iron gates at the front of the little walkway to our house which they would keep bolted, and I know that sounds like drastic action, but they were at the end of their tethers and didn't know what else to do.

Even that didn't rein me in. I would try and climb up the wall of our roof terrace to get out over the other side. Or I would go and stand at the gate and beg strangers passing by to go and get me some vodka. That didn't always work, though. One time I was standing at the gate and I saw someone approaching.

'Excuse me,' I said, as he headed towards me, 'could you do me a favour? If I give you some money, will you go and get me a bottle of vodka from the little shop round the corner?'

He looked at me and said, 'Linda, I've come to see you to see if I can help.'

It turned out he was from an alcohol crisis group who had been contacted by the family . . . so that backfired.

By the Christmas period of 2018, the situation was intolerable. The police had been called to the house on quite a few occasions as I'd been going to the gate and screaming, 'Help! I've been kidnapped! They won't let me out!'

The neighbours would hear the commotion and call the police, who came round to check if everything was OK. When they were here, I'd laugh it off and make out that it was just a bit of a domestic or a joke I'd been having. Of course no one has been kidnapped, officer! There's nothing to worry about here! But then it would be in the papers the next day. I don't know who was tipping the reporters off. It can only have come from the police themselves, I suppose, which is pretty low, isn't it?

Once the press got a whiff that there was trouble, there were paps outside my door the whole time, waiting to get a shot of me at my lowest ebb. I really wasn't well and Mark was at his wits' end, doing everything he could to try and help me. But there was no helping me, not for a long time. And the last thing any of us needed were the paps hanging about.

We had a big row with one of them one day as I was watering my plants on our little Juliet balcony. This young bloke drove past on a bike and he said, 'Did you know there's a load of photographers taking pictures of you down here?'

It made me feel like I was being spied on in my own home. I said I wanted to get out and so my sister, who was round at the time, said we'd go out for a drive. We got in the car and then realized this black Audi was following us. It was the pap.

My sister is quite good behind the wheel whereas I'm Britain's Worst Driver – that's a title I officially won on a TV show in 2003, as a matter of fact.

Tina was going round and round up by the Arsenal, trying to shake him off, and it was dangerous. Every time Tina tried to get away, he'd put his foot down in pursuit.

Eventually she'd had enough and so she stopped the car and got out.

She said to him, 'What are you playing at? My sister's not well. Leave her alone!'

He shouted back, 'You're nothing but f***ing scum!'

She took down his number plate and we phoned the police, who apparently went round and cautioned him.

I was spending whole days crying and I looked absolutely terrible, really skinny like a skeleton. When I look back at the pictures from that time, I'm horrified. It was as if I was at death's door with hollowed-out cheeks and lines etched across my face.

Even on family trips out with the grandkids, my mind was fixated on getting hold of alcohol. We went to see *Nativity!* at the Hammersmith Apollo and I said to Lauren I was popping to the toilet.

'Don't drink, Mum,' she warned.

I didn't have any money on me anyway because they wouldn't let me have access to cash in case I sneaked off and bought alcohol. So instead, I drank the dregs from other people's glasses of wine left on the bar or tables.

How bad is that? But I didn't care. All I wanted was to get pissed so I could sleep.

Christmas is ruined

Lila had her Christmas carol concert and the family told me I wasn't allowed to go, because they couldn't trust me to stay sober. Mark said if I went, he'd put me in the car and bring me straight home again.

I told them they couldn't stop me going, so I went round to the school on foot, and I think because no one wanted to cause a scene they let it go. I was actually OK that evening because I hadn't drunk beforehand, but I had a skinful when I got home.

I destroyed that Christmas Day for everyone by managing to get absolutely paralytic drunk and passing out. Downstairs in our cinema room we had a sofa and behind it we kept bottles of champagne that I'd been gifted over the years. None of us drank champagne so it was always just left there for us to take as presents to other people's birthday parties. But I drank every last drop that Christmas Day. I wasn't bothered what it was I was drinking as long as it got me completely blind drunk.

Lauren had to take full charge of the dinner – a job which had always been mine but I was incapable of doing now. Before people had even finished their dinner, I was emptying their plates into the bin and trying to clear everything away, and then I went upstairs and blacked out on the bed.

The most heart-breaking moment of this whole period came when Lauren told me I couldn't look after Lila and Betsy any more. If Louis or Bobbie Girl were with me, she said it would be OK, but I wasn't allowed to be with them on my own. The final straw for her had been when I'd had the kids in the car and had left them there while I stopped to run into a shop. I thought it would be OK because I could see the car the whole time, but Lauren happened to be walking along the street at that moment and she saw the kids on their own. She was furious with me. I'd left the keys in the ignition and she was saying someone could have driven off with them in the back.

I can see why she was so mad now, but at the time I was all over the place and making lots of bad decisions. Lauren said she was becoming concerned about me doing harm to myself in front of them. I was crying all the time and that wasn't good for the girls to witness. She didn't want them to be exposed to any of that; it wasn't fair. Some days I'd walk into a shop with Lila, buy a little bottle of vodka and then secretly drink it when she wasn't looking, which feels awful admitting to.

I totally understood Lauren and Steve's decision and accepted they were right. But it was still devastating to hear, because I love those girls more than anything else in the world. I was behaving in ways which were so far removed from who I was. I might as well have been a different person.

There was an awful day when poor Bobbie Girl thought she'd killed me. I knew there was a plate in Louis's room which would need washing and my OCD was making me anxious about it. So I knocked on his door to get it.

He was still eating off it but in my head I needed to wash it. We started to tussle a bit over this plate when Bobbie came along the landing and tried to get me to back off and, before I knew it, I was fighting the pair of them, trying to punch my way past. In the struggle I fell down the stairs. I was OK apart from banging my head quite badly, but for a few seconds Bobbie thought I was dead. She was sobbing uncontrollably.

If you had told me a few months before that I'd be physically fighting with my kids, I would never have believed you. And yet here we were.

At this point the family were having discussions about getting me sectioned under the Mental Health Act. I was suicidal and they were frightened. I was frightened too. They decided against it in the end because they knew I would hate it and, besides, I was willing to go back into treatment voluntarily. We couldn't carry on like this and I knew that. I had to have professional help otherwise the unthinkable was going to happen.

The family secured me a place at the Nightingale Hospital in London and I went there, not really knowing if I'd ever come home again.

I hated myself. I told myself I was just a burden to Mark and the kids and that I was ruining all their lives.

I couldn't even be trusted with my own grandchildren. That's when I really started to think I'd be better off dead. At least without me around they'd be able to get on with their lives and wouldn't have to worry about who was going to be looking after me.

I told the Nightingale staff that I wanted to kill myself and so I was put on a suicide watch with someone sitting outside my bedroom door the whole time. I thought about how I could do it and considered saving my diazepam up and taking them all in one go. I imagined getting a knife and slashing my wrists.

I had started self-harming. The staff did their best to make sure I didn't have access to anything I could use to do it, but someone who is determined to hurt themselves will figure out a way, and I managed to find things which would work. I'd even use the plastic knives and forks, and I became very skilled at concealing what I was doing because there's basically someone watching you wherever you go. I've still got the marks all up my arm. It makes me shudder when I catch sight of them – they are a reminder of how horrific things got.

I was trapped in a hospital bedroom, where death felt like the only way to escape the pain I was in. I wanted nothing more than to die. I woke up each morning and didn't know how I was going to get through the day ahead. Every day felt like a year.

I didn't want to live like this. I hated what I was putting my family through and thought they'd be better off without me. I thought I was never going to be normal again. This was it – I'd hit rock bottom and I had no idea how I was going to crawl my way back up again.

I'd throw stuff out of the window. That became a bit of a thing. I threw clothes out and toiletries and, because of my OCD, anything I thought might have germs on. I chucked my hairdryer one day and I'm lucky it didn't take someone out below with the force.

I tried to escape so many times, but I was never going to manage it. The security would always catch me and take me back while I was kicking and screaming. I was so heavily medicated I wasn't able to think straight.

Lesley came to visit me while I was in there and I used to try and run out with her on to the street as she was leaving.

'I'm coming home with you, Les,' I'd say, pleading with her.

'You can't, Linda. You're not well; you need to stay here and get better.'

She was such a tower of strength for me while I was in there. Lesley might be like a little princess but she's the sort of person you need on your side in a crisis. I know she'll be there for me no matter what.

Move to the Priory

I had so much love and support on the outside, although I wasn't in a position to appreciate it until much later. All the *Loose* lot – Nadia, Kaye, Stacey and Jane – phoned Mark and the kids every day to check on me. Janet Street-Porter did too, and I remember my sister saying, 'I thought she was hard as nails!' But she's got a soft side has Janet. She's a real darling.

After a few weeks in the Nightingale, one of the nurses suggested I was well enough to go into the outside world for a walk and a cup of coffee. I was so happy to be getting out but also felt quite vulnerable because I knew it was a test and I was far from one hundred per cent.

While we were out, I asked if we could pop into Marks & Spencer and while the nurse was having a little browse, I went up to the alcohol counter, asked for a bottle of rum and then immediately started necking it right there in the middle of the shop. I didn't care who saw me.

The nurse came running over (as did the M&S security because I obviously hadn't paid for it) and I was hurriedly taken back to the clinic where I stayed for another month.

By the time I went home in March, I was feeling a bit stronger, but it was only after checking into the Priory that things started to improve and I saw glimmers of hope for the first time. I'd been on such strong doses of the meds at the Nightingale, but at the Priory they said they were going to work to reduce what I was on.

It was Dr Neil Brener there who really helped me. He was the first person to consider that it might be the diazepam that was causing a lot of the issues, so he took me off that and introduced sertraline instead, which I responded to much better. And then at night I'd have quetiapine, which is an antipsychotic drug, and that worked for some reason. My sleeping improved and my state of mind felt a lot calmer and clearer.

I felt safe at the Priory. Everyone there was given a job to do, so you might be loading the dishwasher or laying the table for dinner every evening. I was allowed to do my washing, which was a big bonus for me. Every morning

I'd be outside the laundry room, waiting for it to open at 8 a.m., and I'd do everyone else's washing for them as well. It was the happiest I'd felt in a long time!

After a couple of weeks, the doctors said I was well enough to have some freedom to go home every now and again, and having that 'escape' was a big part of my overall recovery. I'd have a few days with Mark and the kids back at the house and then head back to the Priory for further treatment.

I started the AA's Twelve Steps while I was in there and I began attending meetings whenever I was out of the clinic. I never felt able to speak, but it helped me being around other people who knew what I was going through. It didn't matter who you were or what you did for a living; we were all the same there.

I'd have counselling sessions and was encouraged to write lots of my thoughts and feelings down, which I found really helped. I've still got my diaries and it feels emotional reading them now because they transport me back to a harrowing time. I had a look through them to help me write this book and it wasn't easy, although they also show me how far I've come since. And that makes me proud.

Recovery

Getting back on track

It goes without saying that the months and months of treatment and care I was having was really costly and we burned through pretty much all our savings to pay for it. You have to pay for all your medication while you're in there and everything is eye-wateringly expensive. I once had a blister on my ear and they prescribed Zovirax and charged way more than I would have paid normally. I'd always been the main breadwinner and had supported everyone my whole career, but for a long time while I was poorly I was unable to work and had no money coming in. The care was worth every penny because it saved my life, but it still left us in some financial difficulty.

Mark has always run several businesses (the kids call him the Secret Millionaire), so he was able to cover a lot of it, and my sister Tina helped out too – I've since paid her back every penny, even though she said she didn't want it. It was important to me to settle up.

Over the next few months I gradually put myself back together again. There was still a lot of work I had to do, even after I'd checked out of rehab, so I would make sure I kept my days full. Even if it was just popping to Tesco to get some shopping in or reading a book, it was keeping me occupied and distracted. If I stayed indoors with nothing to do, that's when I would feel the depression creeping back.

Return to work

Towards the end of 2019 I went into ITV to discuss my return to work. I sat down in the meeting and was asked if I felt ready to come back. I told my bosses I was, and I really meant it; I knew I was strong enough.

They then asked if I was still drinking, which was a fair question and one that needed to be asked.

I said I hadn't touched a drink for nearly a year.

We decided I would come back first as a guest, basically to explain to viewers, who had been kept in the dark about my prolonged absence, where I'd been for the last year. I asked if the panel that day could be my best Loose Women, the ones who understood me more than anyone, and they agreed that it would be Nadia, Kaye, Stacey and Jane.

I knew going back to the studio was going to be hard and I didn't sleep a wink the night before, worried that I was going to let everyone down. I didn't know how people were going to react and whether they'd think it was something I'd brought on myself.

The kids had bought me a lovely blue top to wear from Topshop and they wanted to come with me to ITV, but I felt like I needed to do this on my own. I was really nervous walking through the doors on 10 January 2020. It was such a familiar place to me and yet today it felt so different. But it was made easier knowing I was going to have Nadia, Kaye, Stacey and Jane by my side.

They came into the dressing room to see me beforehand and we all had a hug. I told them I wanted to be really honest and so they could ask me anything and I would tell them exactly what had happened. They told me if it ever got too difficult, they would pull me through. I knew they would too.

Kaye introduced me as 'a very special Loose Woman and a dear friend' and I came out to the audience applauding and warm hugs from the girls. The whole thing went really well and it felt like a huge relief finally telling my story, speaking my truth and letting people know where I'd been all this time.

The response from viewers was so positive and I'll always be grateful for how they welcomed me back. I had loads of messages saying they had wondered where I'd been and had been worried about me and were so pleased to see me back and looking well. People said thank you for speaking up, and it made me even more convinced that going public was the right thing to do. There should be no shame in mental health issues and I think it can only be positive that more people feel able to share their experiences these days. It's down to brave women like my *Loose Women* friend Denise Welch, who has paved the way for others to open up.

I didn't know where things would go from there, but the next day I got an email from ITV asking me to come back as a panellist for two days the following week. I was overjoyed, because I honestly hadn't been sure if I still had a future on the show.

I thought, *Thank God for that. I have a job now.*

Making amends

Jane Moore asked me to do an interview with her for the *Sun*, which I agreed to because I trusted her. I got paid for it as well, which helped pay off some of the debts I'd racked up and also made sure I was able to treat the kids. They didn't want treating and have never asked me for money, but it was something that was important to me to do.

There's no going back now. I'm doing really well and I'd say I'm back to where I was before this nightmare began. I've been off all my medication since the end of 2020. I was reducing the sertraline anyway and then a couple of times I forgot to take it completely and I felt fine. I was still taking the quetiapine, but when I ran out of that I thought I'd try and see if I could manage without it and I've been all right.

My OCD is much better. I still have two baths a day and I'll always be a clean freak, but it doesn't feel overwhelming any more. I don't even go to AA meetings these days, which I know wouldn't be the right thing to do for a lot of people and I will go back if I ever feel myself slipping. But I haven't had a drink since that episode in M&S with the rum and I'm absolutely fine to be around alcohol. I'm never tempted.

People used to make sure there was no alcohol in sight whenever I went round to their house and checked with Mark ahead of social events about how to handle the situation, but it's not a problem. I'm not interested in it. I've been to loads of showbiz dos, parties and on lots of holidays and it has never entered my head to have a drink.

I stick to tea, sparkling water or sometimes I'll have a virgin piña colada because that makes me feel quite grown-up. I don't actually think the booze was ever the issue. It was a symptom of a much bigger problem and I was using it to self-medicate.

The only thing I can't get over is the guilt about what I put my family through. It was horrendous for all of them and I hate what it did to us. We've spoken about it at length because I think it's important that we're all honest over how it's affected us, and they've told me they didn't think they were ever going to get me back. They thought that was it; they'd lost their mum for ever. They were so scared. I don't think I'll ever be able to forgive myself for that.

Lila says to me, 'Remember when you weren't well and used to cry all the time?'

I say, 'I do remember, darling. But I'm all right now.'

And she'll say, 'I'm glad you're back to yourself, Nanny.'

The first time Lauren and Steve left me on my own with the girls again was really emotional. I was away with the four of them at a caravan in Clacton and Lauren said she was going out for a drink with Steve and would I mind staying in with the kids?

Would I mind?! I was ecstatic. And so thankful that she trusted me with those precious girls again. Now I look after them all the time and there's nothing I love more than picking them up from school and having Betsy come running up to me and giving me the biggest cuddle. There's no feeling that can match that.

Getting back to work played a huge part in my recovery. I took fun jobs like *Pointless Celebrities* with Andrea McLean and I did *Celebrity Supermarket Sweep*. I also narrated the documentary series *Bad Girls Behind Bars*, and it all helped strengthen the sense of purpose and self-worth that I'd lost for so long.

And although *Loose Women* had gone off air when the first Covid lockdown came into force in March 2020, we came back after a five-week break and it was a lifesaver for me. Being able to go into work and see my friends, even if we had to socially distance ourselves from each other, gave me a little slice of normality when it felt like the world was ending. And it played a big part in keeping my mental health in balance.

Because Pauline is happier out of the public eye these days, I've been doing more work stuff with Lesley, who still thrives on life in the spotlight. I love her so much for that; she is an absolute force of nature. We've done *Who Wants to Be a Millionaire?*, which was great, but one of the best jobs we've ever done together was *Celebrity Coach Trip*, which we filmed in September 2021.

She phoned me up and said, 'They've asked us to do *Coach Trip*. What do you reckon?'

I asked where it was and she said Portugal.

Sold! I jumped at the chance, especially as since Covid I'd not really been anywhere, so I was itching to get away. These shows don't really pay very much in terms of a fee, but they get you away on a freebie jolly and you know how I love my sunshine and holidays.

On the way to the airport the morning we were leaving, Lesley called me.

What now? I thought as I answered the phone, because there's always something.

'Linda, I've hurt my back, very badly,' she said solemnly.

'Oh yeah?' I said. Lesley is prone to exaggeration so I take most things she says with a pinch of salt.

'Yes, so you'll have to carry my luggage for me.'

That figured.

'How many cases have you got?' I asked.

'Two cases and two bags.'

Trust her to have double the allowance. I only had one case and a small carry-on.

Anyway, there's me at the airport, loaded up like the little donkey with six bags in total while Lesley flounces off in front.

'Come on, Linda! We'll miss the flight!' she called to me as I struggled, huffing and puffing behind her, trying to keep up.

When we got out there, we had to do these challenges like parasailing and being dragged around the sea on this inflatable doughnut, and Lesley did all this without a single mention of her injured back.

'Your back ain't hurting now, is it?' I said to her. 'Seems f***ing fine to me.'

That's Lesley all over. She's always been a little madam.

I nearly killed myself on that giant rubber doughnut when I let go of the handles and came flying off at top speed. I almost lost my swimming costume as well and I had to make the director swear on his life that they wouldn't use that footage.

Seriously, though, I was in awe of Lesley on that trip. She has the energy of a woman half her age. She never shirked a challenge and she had no trouble keeping up with the young ones. She's made of the toughest of stuff that one.

We really got on with the *Geordie Shore* stars Sophie Kasaei and James Tindale who were on the coach with us from the start. I didn't really know who they were, but I'd heard of *Geordie Shore*. I loved the drag queens Ginny Lemon and Sister Sister; they were great fun. I kept in touch with them and have been to see them at the Palladium since the show.

Me and Lesley weren't bothered about winning but we were having such a good time we wanted to stay in for as long as possible. I think some of the contestants got the hump about that. The two girls from the Honeyz were lovely, but they were desperate to win, and unfortunately for them they were practically the first two out.

We didn't know who the coach was going to pick up en route so it was always a complete surprise. When Nancy Dell'Olio came on board I joked to Lesley that it was a bit of competition for her. I said, 'Oh, here we go. She's got nicer clothes than you, love.'

Nancy, who was paired with Chesney Hawkes, actually made Lesley look low maintenance. That's no mean feat, believe me.

None of us could understand what she was doing on the show. She didn't want to do any of the activities and she'd be wearing all her Valentino and Versace pieces, which were lovely to look at but completely out of place on a show like *Coach Trip*.

She was really generous, though. Ginny once said to her that the kaftan she was wearing was gorgeous and she said, 'Oh, you can have it.'

I was kicking myself that I hadn't said it first because that kaftan was beautiful. All her clothes were. She spent a lot of time in the toilet. I presume putting her make-up on, but she never joined in anything and she was voted off after just three days.

No one was more surprised than me and Lesley when we were crowned the winners of the series. We were so happy about it, though. I never win anything!

A Christmas special without Pauline

ITV had commissioned a Christmas special of *Birds of a Feather* and I couldn't wait. It was the show I loved more than any of the rest after all.

There was only one problem. Pauline had quit.

I'm not going to lie and say me and Lesley weren't disappointed with her decision. Of course we were. We were gutted and we couldn't imagine going on without her. We were a trio – how could it possibly work without any one of us? But at the same time as all that sadness, there was acceptance and understanding too. She didn't want to do it any more; her reasons were completely valid and I totally respected her decision.

I had a feeling she was building up to telling us. You don't have a friendship spanning more than fifty years and not get a sense for what each other is thinking. So it wasn't a huge shock when she sat me and Lesley down over lunch in early 2020 and said she didn't want to do the Christmas special that year. Or any other episodes which might follow for that matter.

'I don't want to act any more,' she said. 'It's not *Birds of a Feather* itself; it's everything. I feel like I'm done with it. I feel bad for you two, but you can go on without me.'

I wasn't sure that we could.

Pauline explained that she didn't want the long hours away from home; she wanted to concentrate on her performing arts academy, and she's got her grandchildren who live nearby – same as me – and she wanted to be around and available to look after them. She'd stopped enjoying the social side of things as well. When we finished work at night, Pauline couldn't wait to get home and put her jarmies on, whereas me and Lesley would go out for dinner or a drink somewhere to wind down.

She told us how she had started to find the twelve-hour filming days really tiring and we all knew that she had never enjoyed the studio days where we had to perform in front of the live audience. For someone who is as brilliant an actress as Pauline, it's really sad how much she doubts her own ability and gets herself so nervous. She hated the tours we did because the nerves would get the better of her and every night she'd be in pieces before we went out on stage. I wish she had more confidence and self-belief, but she's always been like that, even when we were kids.

Laurence and Maurice thought she'd change her mind nearer the time and get on board with the Christmas special, but I knew that she wouldn't. Although she was sorry that it was letting us down, she had also been clear and adamant, and there was no way back.

It wasn't just a shame for us but for the industry as a whole because Pauline is such a huge talent. We knew that when the news was announced it would set the rumour mill going that there had been some big fallout. Sure enough, the headlines were all very predictable, saying there was a 'feud' and 'bad blood' and that she'd quit because we were no longer speaking. It's such bulls***.

We tried to ignore it, but it was difficult when it was all we were ever asked about and it drove us mad. Me and Lesley had *This Morning* on the phone asking us to come on and talk about the 'fallout' which didn't exist in the first place. We turned down all the offers because we've been in the industry long enough to know that talking about anything, even to deny it, only adds fuel to the fire. Most of the time, if you just leave things alone and refuse to entertain them, they'll die a death. And anyway, we knew the truth, so did it really matter what anyone else thought?

Me and Pauline might not be working together any more, but our friendship will outlive all of that. We have been there for each other through thick and thin and for every single major life event, whether that's been break-ups, weddings, birthdays, motherhood, divorces, anniversaries or funerals. She always joked that she let me do things first and if it worked out, she'd follow. So I had Lauren and then she had her daughter Emily. Then I had Louis and she had Charlie. After that, I had Bobbie Girl and she said, 'Nah, you're all right. I'll stop now!' But the kids are all really close as well; they've grown up together.

We have supported each other through some extremely

tough times – she was there for me when both my parents died as I was for her when she lost her mum Hetty, who I loved very much, to cancer in 1989, just before *Birds of a Feather* took off. It's sad that her mum never got to see what a success Pauline made of her life.

We've both had our fair share of tragedy to contend with. Her sister Kitty had a kidney transplant and died not long after. Pauline was really close to her and I was there for her to lean on while she grieved. She did the same for me when I lost my mum and dad and later when I fell ill myself.

The decision she made about *Birds of a Feather*, however much I wished she felt differently, was never going to come between us. There is simply too much history there and our relationship is bigger and stronger than any TV show.

Just me and Les

After a lot of deliberation, me and Lesley decided to go ahead and do the Christmas special without Pauline. We were nervous about whether we'd be able to pull it off, just the two of us, but when we saw the scripts, we knew we'd be all right. Sharon (and therefore Pauline) was still very present in the episode, just not on screen, and the storyline had her stranded on a cruise ship off the coast of Costa Rica thanks to Covid. Tracey and Dorien talked about her all the time and when I said how much I missed her I meant it in real life too.

Paul O'Grady was signed up to be in it as Dorien's

latest love interest, but that didn't work out, so he was replaced by Les Dennis and I think he was really good.

The writers made it very current with lots of references to the lockdown and the pandemic, and it went down well – we were still getting millions of viewers more than thirty years after the very first episode back in 1989. Not many shows can say that and I feel very proud about what we achieved.

We loved making it, but to be perfectly honest I think that's us done now. People ask us if and when it's coming back all the time, and maybe we'll make a big return in another ten years with Sharon, Tracey and Dorien all in an old people's home together. That could work! But in all seriousness that Christmas episode felt like the last one and I think it probably will be. There was something very final about it. And although it was fine to do that special with just me and Lesley as a one-off, I couldn't contemplate doing a full series without Pauline. It just wouldn't be right.

In the spring of 2022 the three of us went out for a lovely lunch together at the swish Delaunay restaurant in central London and it felt so good to be back together. We'd been out for lunches before then, but this time we decided to make a bit of a stand against the reports of a rift. As I said earlier, we didn't want to address them directly, but sometimes a picture can say a thousand words, can't it? So we had our photo taken together and I got Bobbie Girl to upload it to my Instagram later on, captioning it: *A lovely lunch with my beautiful friends.*

It was our way of saying 'There you go, that'll shut you up!'

And it did.

New Beginnings

The truth about my marriage

OK, cards on the table. I'm very aware that there have been rumours circulating about my marriage for a while now but I've never commented on them. Until now.

The challenges of the last few years have meant doing a lot of soul-searching about the future. And it's fair to say that after more than thirty years of marriage, me and Mark have drifted apart. I think it started when the kids left home and suddenly there was just the two of us. I told you before that we don't have an awful lot in common, and I suppose with the children gone and the empty house, those differences became quite exposed. All the kids still live locally and Bobbie Girl comes round after work most days, so it's not like any of them are ever far away. But it's not the same. The house feels so quiet without them and all their friends who used to fill it with noise and fun.

When a marriage ends, it's always sad – me and Mark have so much shared history and there is still a lot of love there. We'll always be connected by our kids, who we adore equally, and for many years we were a fantastic team. But I do feel I've been given a second chance at life and I need to make sure I spend it being as happy as possible, and if that means a fresh start on my own, then I have to seize it.

Being completely honest, I'm not sure what the future looks like exactly – I wish I could tell you more but it's all a bit up in the air. What I do know is that I'm not interested in finding anyone else. That's not what this is about. I'm not scared about being single either – I have enough family and friends to make sure I'm always supported and I'll never be lonely.

I've had a couple of offers to take me out but I've said no thank you. I just don't feel the need and I don't even know what I'd do on a date these days. Denise Welch bought me a vibrator, though. She was shocked to hear that I'd never had one before and thought she'd help me out now I'm on my own and not getting any, so she left one in my dressing room. I walked in to find this great big pink thing sitting there on my table.

I took it home and got it out the box to have a closer look, but I wouldn't have had a clue how to use the thing. Not my cup of tea.

I put it back in the packaging and gave it to Lauren to pass on to one of her mates. I don't need a man and I don't need a vibrator either. I get plenty of affection from my family and I want to focus on looking after myself.

A girl's best friend

I've got my gorgeous French bulldog Dolly for company as well, and I love her with all my heart – just as much as the grandkids! I got her from Battersea Dogs & Cats Home in early 2022 and the joy she's brought to my life is priceless. She has the sweetest nature and I felt a connection with her as soon as I laid eyes on her.

Lila and Betsy are obsessed with her. Those girls are dog mad. Their other nan, Nanny Brenda, has a dog called Bailey and they'd been desperate for me to get one too. Well, I couldn't let Nanny Brenda have one up on me, could I? So I took the two of them with me to Battersea and they were included in the whole process. In your face, Nanny Brenda!

Dolly was one of five Frenchies taken to Battersea and she was the runt of the litter, bless her. She can't see properly out of one eye but she's perfect to me. Dolly has become such an important part of my life now and so central to my happiness that I can't imagine a world without her. She causes me plenty of problems as well, mind! She has accidents all over the house, which isn't good for someone like me with OCD. I spend a lot of time on my hands and knees scrubbing the carpet. I tried to train her but maybe I did it wrong by putting the absorbent mats everywhere rather than just by the back door. Someone said I might have confused her about where she's allowed 'to go' but who knows?

She can be destructive too. I bought a stunning pair of FitFlops when I was in Cyprus, all covered in sparkling sequins – I loved them, they were like my posh shoes. I came back after filming *Loose Women* one day and immediately saw a trail of sequins going up the stairs . . .

One shoe was intact and perfect, but the other one was completely demolished. Those sequins were coming out of Dolly's arse for days.

Turning sixty-five

I managed to get lost on the way to my own sixty-fifth birthday party. It was only ten minutes away from where I live but I drove and because I have no sense of direction I ended up in the city. I was driving round Spitalfields while everyone was waiting for me to arrive. Louis had to come and find me in his car so I could follow him back.

The kids had organized it all at a restaurant which isn't posh or anything; it's just really nice and homely. Everyone from *Loose Women* was there, from the runners to the producers, and then all my friends and family – there must have been about a hundred of us and we had such a good night. I'd bought loads of wine for everybody but I was happy with my pot of tea. Wherever I go, I manage to get a cuppa.

We had a Motown singer and Brenda Edwards got up and did a few numbers as well and these are memories I'll treasure for ever.

I got so many generous gifts – candles, lovely scarves, beautiful jewellery. Brenda got me a gorgeous peace lily plant, which has grown ever so nicely in my lounge ever since and is a great reminder of a very special evening.

It all went on until about one or two in the morning and then I drove everyone home afterwards.

I still can't believe I'm sixty-five. In my head I'm half my age, although my body thinks differently. I went to watch Lila in her school play recently and most people were sitting on the floor. If I'd sat down there, I'd have never got up again. But on the whole and all things considered, I'm not bad for my age.

Trying new things

We never know what lies ahead for us and sadly I've seen too many times how life can change in a split second. Seeing people like Brenda Edwards and the Kinsella family inspires me to make the most of every minute, and I'm determined to give everything a go. If I can't do it, I can't do it, but at least I'll have tried. I'm doing more now in my sixties than I've ever done, because the way I look at it is that I might not get the chance to do this again.

Bobbie Girl bought the two of us a five-day trip to Miami for my birthday, and when we got there she had all these things booked for us because she's really organized like that.

One of the excursions was to swim with sharks, which was something she really wanted to do. I told her I'd go out in the boat with her but I wasn't getting into the sea with the sharks. F*** that.

Anyway, there was a cage to go in, but the captain said the type of sharks in there weren't dangerous so it was fine to just swim amongst them. Bobbie went straight in there and I was videoing her but still wasn't tempted to join her.

I asked the captain where the toilet was and he pointed to the sea.

'In there,' he said.

'In where?'

'In the ocean.'

So I had a choice. Either get into the shark-infested waters or wet myself on the boat. I chose the sharks and so I ended up swimming with them after all. I'm so glad I did.

Grabbing life

I'd wanted to parachute out of the aeroplane on *I'm a Celebrity* because I thought it would be the safest way to do it. They weren't going to let you die on television, were they? But it wasn't my half of the group who got to do that and so I was a bit disappointed.

Knowing how much I'd wanted to do it, the *Loose Women* girls bought me an aeroplane jump for my sixtieth birthday and I was terrified but worked hard to psyche myself up. I hadn't been able to sleep the night before, and the kids were winding me up telling me it was ridiculous a woman of my age doing that and I was going to end up breaking my leg or even worse when I landed. But I'd said I would do it and I didn't want to let anyone down.

I met the crew at Waterloo station in the morning and they warned me that the weather wasn't looking too good so we might have to reschedule for the following day. I told them there was no way I'd be able to pluck up a second load of courage the next day too, so it was today or not at all.

We got the train to somewhere near Stonehenge where they had everything ready for me and there was no going back. We went up in the plane and it was a really cold, cloudy day and they kept on opening the hatch ready to jump and then putting it back down again. I just wanted it to be over.

Before I knew it, I was pushed out of the plane and was plummeting to the earth. I had someone on my back who had done something like 700 jumps, so he knew what he was doing, but for the first few seconds when I was in freefall, I thought, *Oh my God, it's not going to open.*

Obviously it did, because I'm here telling you about it, and once the parachute comes out and you shoot up before flying back to the ground, it is the most exhilarating experience. And it's over in about six minutes from start to finish.

That's what life is for, isn't it? Grabbing by the horns and making the most of whatever time we have left. That's exactly what I intend to do from now on. I've seen enough tragedy in my time and I've got the battle scars to prove it, but I'm still here and all the challenges that have been thrown at me over the last few years have given me a fresh outlook on life, which means I'm saying yes to everything. An experience like this does fundamentally change you – how could it not?

So that might mean taking some risks. It might mean pushing myself out of my comfort zone. It might even mean swimming with a few sharks or jumping from the odd plane, but that's what living is all about, isn't it?

Retirement? Never!

I look at people like Gloria Hunniford, Janet Street-Porter and Lesley Joseph, still working well into their seventies and eighties, and I want to be like them. I can't think of anything worse than retiring and being stuck at home doing my gardening. I'd be bored out of my mind! In any case, I need to keep working because I've got parking tickets to pay off!

I'm not bothered about the money really. If it's good

fun to do, I'll do it even if the money is peanuts. Staying active and doing what you love is what keeps you young. I want to carry on pushing myself, I want to travel – I want to explore Italy and I want to do it in style.

I know I'm more known as myself and a 'celebrity' thanks to *Loose Women*, but I'll always be an actress first and foremost. It's what I've done since I was ten years old and it's where my heart is.

In 2023 I did a few days on *Bermondsey Tales*, which was a proper production with lovely caterers and people looking after us in wardrobe.

A little stint on *EastEnders* would be nice. One of the producers came up to me at the NTAs recently and asked why I'd never been on the show.

'Because you ain't f***ing asked me!' I told him.

And he said they would have to do something about that. So you never know! I think I'd be quite good on there, don't you?

I have so much to look forward to. Bobbie Girl and her partner Scott got engaged recently so we've got a wedding to plan. Bobbie's got expensive tastes so it's going to be a big one. I hope Scott has braced himself!

I've never felt more confident in myself or more at ease with who I am, how I look and what others think of me.

I'm so grateful for the life that I have, for all the opportunities which continue to come my way and for the people who love and support me unconditionally.

I've got a beautiful family, fabulous friends, a job I adore and, after a long road to recovery, I've got my health.

How could I possibly ask for more than that?

I feel like the luckiest woman in the world.

Acknowledgements

There are so many people I need to thank for supporting me through everything I do.

To my children, Lauren, Louis and Bobbie Girl, who I love with all my heart. I am so proud of you. You all work so hard and have grown up to be kind, caring and with strong principles. I couldn't have wished for a better family.

To Lila and Betsy who bring me so much happiness. I love being your Nanny Linda. How did I get so lucky?

And to my husband Mark who is an amazing dad.

Tina and Debbie, my two lovely sisters, and Jackie (who is a sister in all but name), thank you for always being there. I couldn't do this without you.

To my mum, Rita, who worked her fingers to the bone and loved me Tina and Debbie more than life itself. I miss you.

Anna Scher, you were my inspiration. You took working class kids off the street and gave us confidence and, in so many cases, careers we could never have dreamed of. You are very much missed by us all.

Lesley and Pauline, what can I say? You are my lifelong friends and always will be. We've made the most incredible memories together and I'm so blessed to have you both in my life.

To Beth Neil, thank you for being so patient and working so hard to make this book happen. Thanks as well to my amazing team at Penguin Random House, especially Fenella Bates, Paula Flanagan and Alan Samson who had faith in me from the beginning.

To Sally Shelford and all my *Loose Women* friends, I can never express enough thanks for always having my back.

Finally, to you, the reader. Thank you for coming with me for this trip down memory lane. I'm forever grateful for your love and support.

Image Credits

Page 1 bottom centre: Evening Standard / Stringer via Getty

Page 2 top centre: © Children's Film Foundation Ltd. / Still Courtesy of the BFI National Archive

Page 4 top centre: Maximum Film / Alamy Stock Photo

Page 4 bottom centre: Maximum Film / Alamy Stock Photo

Page 5 top right: AJ Pics/ Alamy Stock Photo

Page 7 top centre: WENN Rights Ltd / Alamy Stock Photo

Page 7 bottom centre: PA Images / Alamy Stock Photo

Page 10 top centre: Robbie Jack / Contributor via Getty

Page 10 bottom centre: Jacky Chapman / Alamy Stock Photo

Page 11 top centre: PA Images / Alamy Stock Photo

Page 11 bottom centre: WENN Rights Ltd / Alamy Stock Photo

All other photographs courtesy of Linda Robson ©